"Ryan McAnany and Molly McAnany recount an extraordinary story of discovery and service; an in-depth, personal, fascinating and largely untold account of a remarkable Florentine named Giorgio La Pira. The book ably demonstrates how individuals change the course ~f ~ and will be of keen interest to ar power, personal diplomacy, i

    Dr. Brent Strathman, Ur
    Santa Barbara

TIED BY A FLORENTINE KNOT

With gratitude to

fondazione giorgio la pira

 FONDAZIONE CR FIRENZE   REGIONE TOSCANA   COMUNE DI FIRENZE   MINISTERO DELLA CULTURA

TIED BY A FLORENTINE KNOT

The American Press on
Giorgio La Pira

Ryan McAnany
Molly McAnany

For the Giorgio La Pira Foundation
Fondazione Giorgio La Pira

New City Press
Hyde Park, New York

Published by New City Press
202 Comforter Blvd.,
Hyde Park, NY 12538
www.newcitypress.com

Tied by a Florentine Knot
The American Press on Giorgio La Pira

Ryan McAnany, Molly McAnany
For the Giorgio La Pira Foundation / Fondazione Giorgio La Pira

Cover design and layout by Miguel Tejerina

Library of Congress Control Number: 2021943584

ISBN 978-1-56548-708-6 (paperback)
ISBN 978-1-56548-709-3 (e-book)
Printed in the United States of America

Contents

Via dei Calzauioli, Florence, Italy, 1960
© Foto Torrini Firenze

Foreword

Giorgio La Pira's work definitely had a global dimension: it was part of a dynamic of the gradual "unity of the Church, unity of the world" toward which mankind is oriented, albeit with a thousand hesitations and difficulties, according to what La Pira called the "teleology of history."

But—one might ask—in the face of his indefatigable work to "break down walls and build bridges," in the face of the hundreds of letters he wrote to the leaders of the entire world, how was all of this perceived outside of Italy and how is it perceived today?

This is the question that prompted the writing of this book. The Fondazione Giorgio La Pira wanted to begin in the United States by researching the type and amount of attention garnered by La Pira from the American press. One only has to consult the *New York Times* archives online to see that the name La Pira appears in several dozen articles.

But it is compelling to not limit oneself—as far as possible—to the big national newspapers, to also take note of whether and how the unprecedented way that the mayor of Florence (later president of the World Federation of United Cities) worked for peace also made it into the local press, which is usually somewhat disinclined to cover international events.

We therefore asked a new friend—Ryan McAnany—to carry out this research, a task requiring a great deal of patience, and to report on the most notable results. He did so scrupulously, seeking all the available information and reporting it impartially, without any "hagiographic" bias, but rather including all the criticisms and negative comments that La Pira's stances and attitudes sparked.

In chapter 1, Ryan himself tells us that he "discovered" La Pira only recently and almost by chance, but that he quickly became fascinated by his life, thought, and work. He tried to read all the information available today in English on the pages of the internet, starting with translations of letters, writings, and speeches by La Pira that the La Pira Foundation was able to post on its website.

So, in a certain sense, this book not only gives an idea of how the American press viewed La Pira—for better or worse—but also of how a modern-day Californian perceives and interprets him. As an accompaniment to Ryan's text, we have decided to also publish the biographical profile of La Pira prepared by the Foundation for the cause of beatification.

The result is a highly readable and interesting book that both the Italian and American public can appreciate. I wish to express my sincerest gratitude to the whole McAnany family. Ryan got them involved in his work, and he pursued it with passion and enthusiasm. In addition, I really hope that this passion and enthusiasm are contagious and that Giorgio La Pira will always be a familiar figure in the United States. We are talking about a man whose example is more topical and crucial than ever, as Pope John Paul II said: "La Pira's experience as a politician and believer was exceptional as he united contemplation and prayer to social and administrative work, giving special preference to the poor and suffering."[1]

Mario Primicerio
Chairman of the La Pira Foundation

Author's Note

The challenge entrusted to me to write a narrative and critical analysis of the American press's perspective of Giorgio La Pira was a difficult but rewarding endeavor. There were many iterations along the way, but my desire to write something meaningful about the complex media interest in this extraordinary individual was the driving force throughout.

Having never even entertained the idea of writing a book, I sought collaboration with my daughter Molly, an undergraduate at the University of California, Santa Barbara, who was studying political science, English, and journalism —the ideal trifecta to facilitate this wonderful project.

Our process began with my extensive research of news sources in the United States. I collected and collated articles and news items that ranged from features of La Pira to photographs with a simple description beneath. We tried to include any article where La Pira's name had been mentioned, no matter how small a part he played in the event it covered. The fact that La Pira's name *is* mentioned as much as it is in the US press over several decades is astonishing, considering his relative anonymity in America today.

With regard to those articles that contained but a few sentences or photos providing virtually no information—as in the case of the meeting between La Pira and the mayor of San Mateo, which was memorialized with only a photo and minimal particulars—we hunted for additional details in an effort to elaborate on those stories and provide context of the period and the possible impetus for the story's coverage in the United States.

Molly and I then analyzed the details of the reporting, bouncing ideas back and forth and eventually arriving at a point where we agreed on the core elements of the article. Instead of providing a linear tale of the life of La Pira, we opted to compartmentalize the fundamental aspects of the man: his time as mayor (chapter 2), his emergence as a world figure (chapter 3), his faith (chapter 4), and lastly, his involvement in the Vietnam conflict (chapter 5).

There were, of course, unexpected challenges. The American press covered La Pira long before the constant news bombardment and easy accessibility we have today. The language, punctuation, and overall style reporters use has changed over time, and there were a few instances where it was difficult to get to the essence of what the writer was trying to convey.

Adding another layer of complexity were the significant contradictions among sources covering Vietnam, something we didn't encounter in the earlier years where multiple publications carried cut-and-paste copies of the same story. It would seem that La Pira's growing significance as a diplomat led to controversy over what actually happened and what was actually said, creating different versions of these events. Our analysis became an interpretation of the differing perceptions of politicians, journalists, world leaders, scholars, and others, as presented based upon the opinions of their own narrative. There were moments in which we accepted: *to each their own truth.*

Not wanting to bore you, the reader, with the minutiae that history can sometimes dole out, we resolved to provide the broad strokes behind certain events so we could highlight the main character, Giorgio La Pira. La Pira was a complex man, and we did not set out to present a comprehensive biography of his life, as there are Italian scholars who have already written many a thesis after studying La Pira for countless years, and who have provided a deeper understanding of his life.

For most Italians, at least in the Tuscan region, La Pira has been a part of their history for as long as they can remember. Many are likely unable to recall the first time that they heard about him. His name and persona are embedded in their culture and minds, body and soul, much like Martin Luther King Jr., John F. Kennedy, and Abraham Lincoln are for us in the United States.

Through this book, we aspire to raise awareness of La Pira's impact on the United States as a diplomat, peace feeler, and spiritual leader. The press reports confirmed his many worthy causes, exhibiting how he worked vigorously to build peace in the world, from its smallest villages to its largest metropolises, from its poorest citizens to its wealthiest inhabitants. La Pira relentlessly attempted to tie a knot that would bind all of humanity together. His life should be known, and his messages of hope, charity, and love should be spread throughout the world.

We hope to introduce La Pira to the younger generations of Americans who continue the fight for equal rights and social justice. It was La Pira who said: "The new generations are indeed like migratory birds, the young are like swallows. They sense the weather, they sense the season. When the spring comes they move in an orderly fashion, driven by an invincible vital instinct—one that shows them the route and the harbours towards the land where spring is in flower."[2]

1

My Discovery of Giorgio La Pira

It astounds me to this day that a family vacation could lead me to discover, and later research, a man that not too many Americans know anything about—especially a man who was embroiled in some of the world's most consequential struggles during the Cold and Vietnam Wars.

I am not a scholar, nor a historian, nor a teacher. I'm not even Italian. Accordingly, when I was asked by Professor Mario Primicerio, president of the La Pira Foundation, to write about the perception of Giorgio La Pira—Italian professor, philanthropist, and global wartime activist—from the perspective of the US press, I was intimidated. Primicerio also asked if I would include my own story of how I came to discover Venerable La Pira and why I became so captivated with the man. The latter was something I was profoundly more comfortable with, as I'd been inundating my family with every informational breakthrough about the life of the mysterious La Pira since I first discovered him.

There have been a few coincidences along the way, leading me to think this was fate. Perhaps I am supposed to tell his story to family and friends, so that they can tell their family and friends and continue to extend the memory of La Pira's extraordinary life beyond Italy's borders.

In 2017, our daughter, the last to leave the nest, was preparing to head off to the University of California, Santa Barbara. To make the most of our time before that eventful day, we booked a family vacation to Italy that summer. The trip provided us with much-needed quality time together, and a temporary distraction for my wife and me from imagining our future as empty nesters.

We had been making our way through Italy from north to south for a couple of weeks by the time we arrived in Florence. The heat was unimaginably oppressive in the afternoons, so we escaped into the small shops along the cobblestone streets for respite. One afternoon, we found ourselves in front of Torrini Fotogiornalismo on Via della Condotta. Vintage black and white photographs of Florence filled the store windows. Once inside, we discovered there were hundreds—perhaps thousands, in retrospect—of quintessentially Italian photographs to browse through. Photos of car races, paparazzi, men in stylish suits, fashionable women, Vespas, people in churches, people sitting in cafes and bars, and of course all the local historical landmarks. There was such an abundance to choose from that at one point we had fifteen or twenty laid out in front of us. My wife and I agreed that we would each pick just one.

The photo that caught my eye, and that I eventually purchased, showed Via dei Calzaiuoli in 1960. It is a powerful image of a bustling city, showing Florentines dressed for the workday, walking, riding their bikes, and shopping. Above their heads, large campaign banners are strung from one building to the next. The banners read: *Democrazia Cristiana, Vota Comunista, Vota Socialismo Democratico, Movimento Sociale Italiano, Votate La Pira,* and *Vota Fabiani.* My wife decided on a photo from 1962 of several young boys on the beach in Calambrone, dressed in white shirts, dark shorts, and cream caps, chasing a single beach ball alongside the ocean with huge smiles on their sun-tanned faces.

One afternoon in early 2019, we finally got around to opening up the photos and had them framed and hung in our home. After a short time, I became intrigued by the political parties on the banners in my photo and began looking into them in more detail. I gathered a basic overview of each party, their history, and the politicians affiliated with them. The fifth banner draped across the street is quite small in the photo, down the street a bit, and reads *"Votate La Pira"*—"Vote La Pira."

The first thing I could find about this La Pira was a Wikipedia entry that gives a somewhat detailed biography of Giorgio La Pira. Now, I had a first name. My search broadened, and the information I learned at each turn intrigued me even more. La Pira was born in Sicily. He belonged to the Christian Democratic Party and was the mayor of Florence from 1951 to 1957 and again from 1961 to 1965. My photo was taken in 1960, leading me to believe that it captured the campaigns for the 1961 election.

At one time La Pira ran an anti-fascist magazine, *Principi*, which he founded and edited while Mussolini was still in power. The story goes that La Pira, having been tipped off that Mussolini's police squad was coming to apprehend him, fled Florence and took refuge in Vatican City. The governorship of Vatican City made La Pira a staff member of *L'Osservatore Romano*, the Vatican newspaper.[3] A year passed before La Pira could return home to Florence. In *Marigold: The Lost Chance for Peace in Vietnam*, by James Hershberg, I found a few pages dedicated to a riveting account of the peace talks La Pira held with Ho Chi Minh in North Vietnam.[4] Although brief, the account gives insight into La Pira's involvement in ending the war in Vietnam.

La Pira was a very pious man who donned the habit of a Dominican Tertiary under the name of Fra (Friar) Raimondo. There are numerous stories of La Pira returning home some days with fewer clothes than he began with, having given away his coat and other items of clothing to the poor while walking. One story describes a policeman who noticed La Pira walking in the rain without a raincoat, leading the officer to give La Pira his to use. When La Pira and the officer met up again at the end of the day, one need only guess what had happened: La Pira had given away the policeman's raincoat to someone in need. He lived in a small room, or cell, as it's called, in the Convent of San Marco in Florence. His cell was furnished with a bed, a bookcase, a desk, and a window that looked down onto the cloisters of the convent. In the colder months, La Pira would stay at a friend's house since his room was not furnished with heat.

Through the Fondazione Giorgio La Pira (Giorgio La Pira Foundation), I also learned that La Pira contributed to the drafting of the Italian Constitution in 1947. Every Saturday, La Pira would visit prisons to assist in court cases, and one of those prisoners even built a miniature wooden ship as a gift to him. La Pira spoke of building bridges as a symbol for unity among peoples. He also, along with the city government, rebuilt physical bridges like the Grazie and Santa Trinita, which were destroyed during the war, and oversaw construction of new ones like the Vespucci Bridge. In 1965, La Pira headed off to Vietnam to meet with President Ho Chi Minh and Prime Minister Pham Van Dong as a designated "peace feeler"; an event that would stir up quite a bit of controversy between the United States and Italy. On July 5, 2018, La Pira became titled "venerable" when Pope Francis confirmed that he had lived a life of heroic virtue.

In photos, I discovered that La Pira was much shorter in stature than I had envisioned. He wore glasses, a fedora, dark suits, and, in almost every photo, a smile with hands outstretched and animated. If there was anyone else in the photo with him, they too would be smiling, unable to resist his infectious personality. According to accounts of the day, La Pira was a riveting orator, and when he taught Roman law at the University of Florence, students would pack an auditorium just to hear the charismatic professor lecture.

By March 2019, a little over two months since I had first discovered La Pira, I was becoming a great deal more interested in the man, perhaps even a bit obsessed. For more than twenty-five years, I have been researching my family history, which made me well versed in research databases and not opposed to long hours spent digging online. These skills served me well as I searched for any link where La Pira was mentioned. At every turn, it seemed as though the documents by or about him became available precisely at that moment so I could find them.

One of my first finds was a handwritten letter by La Pira, which I purchased from an Italian auction site. The letter was written in late 1959 and is addressed to a Mr. Borsieri. The letter and the envelope are in great condition, but I treat them very gingerly, with the respect I feel they deserve. This was when my correspondence with the La Pira Foundation—and my friendship with its president, Professor Mario Primicerio—began. I shared each of my discoveries with them to authenticate the documents and learn the context of each letter, photo, and event. I also inquired about becoming a member of the foundation, but unfortunately, under Italian law, that isn't possible, since I'm not an Italian citizen.

From the Oregon State University archives, I obtained copies of La Pira's correspondence with a man named Linus Pauling, in which La Pira congratulates the other man on receiving the Nobel Peace Prize and invites him to Florence. The archivist also sent a copy of a flyer from a peace parade and rally for Vietnam on Fifth Avenue, which lists La Pira as an expected speaker.

And again, I stumbled upon a few historical items that had just recently been posted for sale online. The first is a Christmas card addressed to the Italian Ambassador to Ghana, Ferruccio Stefenelli, with La Pira's signature at the bottom. The other items are original press photos of La Pira. The photos are just wonderful, really showing how La Pira could be so animated with his hands and, of course, always wearing his radiant smile. Handwritten information on the back of each photo details when the photo was taken and who else was captured in it. According to the seller, he had just unearthed the photos a week prior, after purchasing multiple boxes from an estate sale in northern Italy.

I came to discover that Professor Primicerio himself, who was then a student at the University of Florence, accompanied La Pira on the trip to Vietnam in 1965. After discovering his lengthy history with La Pira, I turned my attention to Primicerio, a professor of applied mathematics at the University of Florence and the first mayor of Florence to be elected by popular vote. I found that Primicerio wrote a book about his experience in Vietnam, published in 2016, entitled *Con La Pira in Viet Nam*.[5] I ordered myself a copy and set about the time-consuming task of translating it page by page via an app.

The relationship between La Pira and Primicerio extends back to the early 1960s. It was while attending a conference in San Vincenzo that the 15-year-old Primicerio first became acquainted with then-Mayor La Pira. Primicerio said, "La Pira visited just for a minute, but his words to the group ring in my ears to this day: you have to pray with the world map on the bedside." He explained in an interview years later, "It meant that prayer must have a global dimension."[6] Primicerio's current role as the head of the La Pira Foundation is a testament to the profound impact La Pira had on the young student all those years ago.

In the months that followed, I continued to research and to email Primicerio any questions I had. He always responded within a few days and, although he was overly gracious with his time, I was still uncertain about how he felt about some American inquiring so profusely into La Pira's life.

When I shared with Primicerio the flyer from the Fifth Avenue peace parade and rally, he said he did not believe that La Pira took part in the rally. But he added, "It comes to mind that a possible source of information would be the heirs or family members of two US peace movement members, Cora and Peter Weiss."[7] However, he cautioned that the couple may have passed, since Peter would be in his nineties and Cora in her late eighties. Feeling privileged to be able to help the foundation, I put on my detective hat and went to work. I was able to obtain Cora Weiss's email address from the author of a piece featuring the Weisses less than a year prior.

My email to Cora was short, asking on behalf of Professor Primicerio if she could provide any letters that they might have to or from Giorgio La Pira. Cora responded promptly and wrote of the extreme admiration she and Peter had and still have for La Pira, expressing her wish that there were "more people like him around today." Cora wrote that she would go through the boxes in her attic to see if she could find anything, but was fairly confident that most of their communication with La Pira was via telephone. She finished by recommending a book, *The Secret Search for Peace in Vietnam*, which includes a captivating chapter detailing when her husband, Peter Weiss, took the midnight train from Strasbourg to Florence to meet with La Pira, who urged him to spread the word among influential Americans to stop the war after his meeting with Ho Chi Minh.[8] I learned sometime after our initial correspondence that Cora did not come across any letters in their archives.

Over dinner one night, I began discussing La Pira, my findings, and my growing relationship with Primicerio with my family. When I came to Cora Weiss and her work in activism, which I knew very little about up to that point, my daughter Molly asked if she could interview Cora for her new podcast *eFEMeral*. After I inquired on her behalf, Cora, being the gracious person she is, wrote back that she loves daughters, having a couple of her own, and would be more than happy to share her story. Granted, the interview was conducted by my daughter, but objectively, it is a captivating interview with an intriguing woman who has spent the majority of her life, much like La Pira, fighting for peace and human rights both domestically and abroad.

My "La Pira Binder" was growing, as I had accumulated quite a bit of info from newspaper clippings, photos, and anything and everything that brought me a bit closer to knowing the true Giorgio La Pira.

In 2019, our daughter was accepted to King's College London for a fall semester abroad. While planning a trip to visit her mid-semester, it occurred to me that, while in London, I'd be only two hours by plane from Florence and it would be foolish not to jump at the opportunity to visit Primicerio and the La Pira Foundation. I reached out to the professor, inquiring if he had time to meet with me and inviting him to dinner to repay him for his months of correspondence. He happily agreed and even added that he would show me the archives of the foundation. I was elated! I was on my own pilgrimage of sorts, back to Florence, the La Pira mecca.

When I arrived in Florence, I made sure to visit Torrini Fotogiornalismo to buy Primicerio a gift for his birthday the next day: a copy of the photograph that sparked my interest in La Pira. On my way back to Hotel Orto de Medici to dress for dinner, I stopped to gaze at the Convent of San Marco. Grabbing a seat on one of the benches in Piazza San Marco, I watched the afternoon sun fade the convent from its hue of ochre and terracotta into a beautiful blue and lemon haze. I took it all in, shaking my head over what had transpired. A photo of San Marco had been my desktop screensaver for close to a year at that point, and here I was, gazing at it in person. The moment was surreal.

For fear of any mishaps that could make me late the following day, I walked down Via Giorgio La Pira to see exactly where the foundation was located. I took a few photos of the foundation's plaque on the wall, then looked up and down the street, imagining a beaming La Pira, arms outstretched, waving to friends and strangers alike.

At dinner, Mario and I indulged in the most delicious Italian meal, replete with hearty red wine and dessert. The professor and I learned about each other's lives, discussing everything from skiing, to politics, to our families, to music. I was happy to learn that Mario is a guitar player like myself and was once in a cover band that toured around Italy.

Of course, our conversation eventually landed on the reason for our meeting: Giorgio La Pira. I began my story about the photo that I purchased two years earlier, something that appeared to intrigue him. Mario shared a couple of experiences about his time with La Pira and the trip he took with him to Vietnam, which was harrowing—simply because of the nature of air travel in those days!

The morning sun was bright when I left the hotel the next day for my very short walk past the Convent of San Marco to the La Pira Foundation. In the foundation's anteroom, which had served as La Pira's office, wooden bookcases line the wall. These bookcases, along with a secured room in the back, contain almost everything written about or by La Pira, according to Mario. It's a vast collection of theses, biographies, letters, and books, all dedicated to the life of La Pira. The archived digitized correspondences that they keep on site are shared with the Convent of San Marco and are being utilized in the current beatification process for La Pira.

The La Pira Foundation's purpose, as it reads on their website, is "the promotion of cultural and social initiatives in the name of Prof. Giorgio La Pira, to pass on his thought and action at national and international level[s] and to preserve and use for cultural purposes" the archives of his work. The website adds that "in 1983, together with the Opera della Regalità and the Convent of San Marco, the Foundation promoted the cause of the beatification of La Pira."[9]

Mario introduced me to two gentlemen at the foundation, Stefano Tilli and Michele Damanti. Stefano's family's involvement with La Pira goes back nearly seventy years—his mother, Antinesca Rabissi Tilli, was La Pira's personal secretary for over thirty years before his death in 1977.

I wished Mario a happy birthday and handed him his present. The first package he opened held copies of the six original press photos I had acquired online. Mario went through each one, taking his time to study the photos and to read the descriptions. He had never seen some of the photos before and shared a bit of information about some of the people pictured with La Pira. Mario, too, observed that La Pira's hands were always moving—a typical mannerism of a Sicilian, he explained. We went through the photos for half an hour or so, until Mario opened the photo that began it all. It brought a smile to both our faces.

We then moved over to one of the computers to look through some of La Pira's letters. The foundation has letters between La Pira and both President John F. Kennedy and Robert Kennedy, which are compelling accounts of Italian-American relations, along with one of the last letters from Pope Paul VI to La Pira in 1977, shortly before La Pira's death.

That day we also received clearance to visit La Pira's cell in San Marco. We were greeted inside the convent by a man with a friendly face. On the left, not too far from the entrance, is La Pira's tomb. I stopped and admired his very modest final resting place, which is flanked by a color portrait of La Pira on a stand. I spent a handful of minutes admiring the tomb, making sure to etch the memory into my mind. Next to La Pira's tomb is a statue of Girolamo Savonarola, which seems only fitting since La Pira was continually compared to the fifteenth-century Dominican friar.

We were shown through a small door behind the altar which opens up into a private chapel. At the top of a set of steep stairs, there is a long hallway with arched wooden doors on both sides. Partway down the hall on the right is La Pira's cell, with his name written in small font. I tried to contain the range of feelings wafting over me as I stood in the room where La Pira slept and worked. The room is small and, like the photos had depicted, contains just a bed, desk, small bookcase, and sink. Mario opened up the wooden shutters on the solitary window to look down over the cloisters. On the desk, there is a copy of La Pira's will under glass; on the wall behind, images of La Pira and Savonarola hang under a small copy of Fra Angelico's *The Annunciation*. The room is as La Pira left it, except for the heater and the two images that stand out on the white-washed walls. I snapped a few photos of what, I'm assuming, not too many people get the chance to see, considering the room is not part of any tour. Back in front of La Pira's tomb, Mario and I thanked and shared a fond farewell with our host and strolled back to the foundation headquarters.

At the corner, Mario stopped to explain that where we were standing, in between the University of Florence and San Marco, was La Pira's favorite spot—the same spot where, just the day before, I had imagined La Pira walking. Inside the foundation, we resumed our places at the table, where I shared with Mario the US newspaper articles I had collected on La Pira. I pulled up some examples on my phone to show him; he seemed surprised that the United States had been covering La Pira as far back as 1949. Mario suggested the publication, through the foundation, of a book about the US perspective of La Pira as well as my story of how I, an American from California, first discovered him. At first, I thought he wanted me to simply make copies of the newspaper articles, but Mario clarified that he wanted me to begin this book as a collaborative project between my daughter and myself. I was a little stunned yet honored to be trusted with such an idea. Within three hours, I had seen so much more than I had ever dreamed. Before I left, I took a photo with Professor Primicerio. I departed with many *grazies* and *ciaos* to everyone, hugged Mario, and stepped out the door into the bright Florence sunlight and onto Via Giorgio La Pira.

2

Early Politics and
Becoming Mayor La Pira

From his tireless work in resolving labor disputes, to advocating against the threats of communism and fascism, to winning the office of mayor in one of the world's most famous cities, Sicilian-born Giorgio La Pira was portrayed as a colorful and controversial character by the US press from the beginning. They covered him closely, pinning several favorable and unfavorable monikers on him that would remain throughout the decades. La Pira's ascetic life at times took the forefront, overshadowing the objectives or accomplishments of his political work. In the end, through all the years he spent as a professor, undersecretary, and mayor, the most indelible label bestowed upon him was "peacemaker."

Having been elected to the post of Undersecretary of Labor in 1948, La Pira was already quite accomplished in his home country by the time the US press wrote of him. On May 25, 1949, La Pira is mentioned, albeit briefly, for what appears to be the first time in a US newspaper. The article in the *Oakland Tribune* detailed the Italian agriculture workers' strike demanding better working conditions and described how "Giorgio La Pira [was] continuing his efforts to renew negotiations between strikers and landowners."[10] Coverage of the five-week farm strike was extensive, as a plethora of American newspaper articles reported on the "communist-led" farm community. This last detail could be why many American journalists had such an interest in covering the situation.[11]

Because he was part of the Ministry of Labor, these localized disputes gave La Pira the tools and agency as a moderator to create a space for dialogue between elites and ordinary people. La Pira, although never mentioned by name in the article about the events in the *Times-Tribune* in Scranton, Pennsylvania, took part in drafting the agreement that settled the violent protest that took the lives of six people.[12] The apparent breakdown of the labor force and maltreatment of the working class by the elites signified a crack in Italy's party state.

In the 1951 mayoral election in Florence, under pressure from religious leaders, La Pira became the Christian Democratic Party candidate. His opponent, incumbent Mario Fabiani, belonged to the Italian Communist Party and was quite critical of the Marshall Plan—officially named the European Recovery Program—which had been signed into action by President Harry S. Truman on April 3, 1948. Fabiani believed that the Marshall Plan was benefiting "the coffers of the 'capitalist' and [was] helping to keep the De Gasperi government of Italy in power," as reported by the *Philadelphia Inquirer* on May 18, 1950.[13]

Before the Marshall Plan was implemented, Fabiani relied on the assistance of the black market to help feed Florentines, stating that "if we tried to smash it, we'd starve the people. . . . You see there just isn't enough rationed food to go around."[14] His criticism was directed toward Alcide De Gasperi, one of the founders of the Christian Democratic Party, who was prime minister of Italy from 1945–1953, and who, in 1948, appointed La Pira as Undersecretary of Labor.

However, the *Santa Cruz Sentinel* wrote on January 2, 1948, that Fabiani welcomed and was "grateful" for the "Friendship Train" that delivered gifts of food from America to the city of Florence.[15] Pre-dating and completely separate from the Marshall Plan, the Friendship Train was a non-governmental program sprung from the idea of American journalist Drew Pearson; it acted as a food bank for post-war Europe, traveling across America and collecting food items from multiple cities along its route. The eleven-day trip began in Los Angeles with twelve freight cars and ended in New York with over 250; thirty-five of those carloads were "donated by New York."[16] The train was welcomed by a ticker tape parade up Broadway, then loaded onto freighters with an expected arrival date in Europe on Christmas Eve.

Paul McC. Warner, editorial page director of the *Philadelphia Inquirer*, believed that there was much confusion over what the Marshall Plan actually did for Americans, aside from costing them billions of dollars. The recovery program, intended to boost the post-World War II economy in Europe, provided the United States more influence over European economic pursuits and thus gave them the upper hand in obstructing communist expansion. The fostering of commerce between the US government and Italy could be why a communist supporter like Fabiani transitioned from a standpoint of cooperation to one of contradiction. However, Italian blue-collar workers also felt that the Marshall Plan was benefiting only the rich. A postal worker in Rome said to McC. Warner: "If you are hungry and can't take care of your family, you don't care where help comes from, as long as you get it. If the communists come along and offer you better things, maybe you listen to them."[17]

Italy's Poorest Man, Mayor of Richest City[18]

During the election campaign of 1951, the *Tucson Daily Citizen* proclaimed Giorgio La Pira "a favorite candidate of both Christian Democrats and their Communist opponents" and said he was the "likely candidate to become mayor," considering his far-left-leaning platform.[19]

On July 5, 1951, the Christian Democratic majority led Giorgio La Pira to become only the second elected mayor of Florence since the end of World War II. The results of northern Italy's local elections were covered by the *Spokane Chronicle*, which ran a piece syndicated by the Associated Press out of Rome sensationalizing the lopsided victory. The article proclaimed that "Premier Alcide de Gasperi's Christian Democrats" delivered the communists a "stinging defeat" by winning 143 cities out of 205.[20]

News of La Pira's mayoral win was repeatedly published throughout the American press, but it was his unconventional approach to life that made the headlines. "Italy's Richest City Honors Poorest Man" was one such headline from August 18, 1951, in the *Bergen Evening Record* headquartered in Hackensack, New Jersey. Journalist Jack Brusini introduced the American reader to the "ascetic" University of Florence professor, Giorgio La Pira.[21]

La Pira was born in the province of Ragusa, in the "poorest town" in Sicily, Brusini noted, and at the age of 20 traveled north to study law at the University of Florence. While a student, La Pira approached the neighboring Convent of San Marco to inquire if the monks would provide him room and board. When "the superior looked at the thin, ascetic face of the young Sicilian," the monk acquiesced.[22]

La Pira "who earlier won a parliamentary seat in the communist stronghold," wrote Brusini, also "teaches one of the driest subjects . . . Italian law," lives in "one of the cells of St. Mark's," "sleeps on a bed without springs," and professes that "poverty is his creed." Brusini wrote of La Pira's astonishing recall, refined oratory skills, and quickwittedness, which resulted in packed auditoriums whenever the professor was to speak. He went on to add that La Pira displayed compassion and generosity by giving the monastery his entire salary as professor and mayor, and was not only generous to the poor, but also to members of opposing political parties.[23]

Political differences never stopped La Pira from having empathy for supporters of the opposition, which at times upset his own political party. He once assisted with the release of two communist youths who had been arrested for starting a fight near the end of a speech wherein La Pira asked those in attendance to "pray for the protection of the Virgin Mary for the City." It was reported by Brusini that after learning of the incident, La Pira rushed to assist, saying that the two youths had "no intention to do any harm"; he pleaded with the police chief to "let them go back to their families." The chief responded that he would do so the next day. Unrelenting, La Pira successfully pressured the police chief for their release and "two hours later La Pira walked the two unhappy youths home."[24]

Multiple newspapers carried the Brusini piece of La Pira's mayoral win but created their own sensational headlines, fixating on the way La Pira conducted his life.

TOWN'S POOREST MAN BECOMES MAYOR
OF ITALY'S RICHEST CITY: FLORENCE'S CHIEF
LIVES IN CONVENT CELL, HELPS POOR,
EVEN AIDS COMMUNISTIC FOES[25]
August 18, 1951 - *Herald-News*, Passaic, NJ

CITY OF FLOWERS IS RULED BY
ITALY'S POOREST CITIZEN[26]
August 18, 1951 - *Press and Sun-Bulletin*, Binghamton, NY

HUMBLE DISCIPLE OF POVERTY
MAYOR OF ITALY'S RICHEST CITY[27]
August 18, 1951 - *Central New Jersey Home News*,
New Brunswick, NJ

ITALY'S POOREST MAN,
MAYOR OF RICHEST CITY[28]
August 18, 1951 - *Daily Record*, Long Branch, NJ

POOREST MAN HEADS
RICHEST CITY OF ITALY[29]
August 18, 1951 - *Argus-Leader*, Sioux Falls, SD

MAYOR OF ITALY'S RICHEST CITY
HAS POVERTY AS CREED[30]
August 19, 1951 - *Gazette*, Cedar Rapids, IA

MAYOR OF FABULOUS FLORENCE
IS THE POOREST MAN IN ITALY[31]
August 24, 1951 - *Beatrice Daily Sun*, Beatrice, NE

A Portrait of the Mayor of Florence

Not long after La Pira was elected mayor, he was visited by the first female recipient of the Pulitzer Prize in journalism, Anne O'Hare McCormick. McCormick had built up an unprecedented resume of interviews during her long and distinguished career, including Benito Mussolini, Adolf Hitler, Joseph Stalin, Winston Churchill, Franklin D. Roosevelt, Éamon de Valera, and Popes Pius XI and Pius XII. Colleagues said McCormick had the astonishing ability to arrive on the scene just as major events were about to unfold, adding that she had a "keen perception" of interviewees' personalities.[32]

In "A Portrait of the Mayor of Florence," published in
the *New York Times* on December 12, 1951, the 71-year-
old McCormick provided a detailed and vivid description
of La Pira's new elevated status. She indicated that the
Florentines were through with communist mayor Fabiani
and instead chose to elect Christian Democrat Giorgio La
Pira, a man who at first appeared somewhat reluctant to
be mayor. McCormick characterizes the 47-year-old La
Pira thus: "The modest little man who looks like an eager
little boy . . . is a deep student of social problems, not in
books but in the backstreets and tenements of Florence."
But she went on to add, "La Pira has dedicated himself to
the 'Christian Revolution,' which he defines as a battle to
restore the dignity of the human being."[33]

It was La Pira's assessment that "the best way to fight
communism [was] to feed [the people] and give them
work." In the interview, McCormick suggested that some
Florentines believed La Pira emulated St. Francis, which
caused the newly elected mayor to smile and shake his
head in disbelief, countering, "The gentleness and love of
St. Francis is sorely needed in our angry age . . . but the
fighting spirit of St. Dominic is also necessary to carry on
'the Christian revolution.'"[34]

McCormick stated that La Pira attacked with "vigor
and enthusiasm" any issues that arose, having implemented more reforms than the previous administration.
She highlighted the "Four Point Program" he had created for his city. The plan of action was to provide more
housing, increase employment, boost public assistance
to the needy, and encourage the arts, because "a city like

Florence cannot live without music, art and beauty,"[35] according to La Pira.

McCormick concluded her piece by remarking on the new administration's shifting of priorities. Moving forward, the "emphasis [was] toward the people irrespective of the party." La Pira sensed communism was finished in the region, but knew that it depended on whether or not he and his party could deliver on their promises.[36]

A city of art

"What can I tell you about Florence? It is a beautiful city: It is one big flower. A superb flower. It looks like a city of art, a castle of a thousand kinds of lace, quick, smooth and magnificent lines. It is truly the land of Dante."[37]

Barely a year into his role as mayor, La Pira was called to assist in halting modern architecture commissions from being erected next to famous landmarks of the Florentine landscape.

New York Times foreign correspondent Arnaldo Cortesi, who lived in Rome, "combined Continental Urbanity with American Journalism" as he told stories of the picturesque Italian lifestyle.[38] Cortesi, a Pulitzer Prize recipient for his distinguished correspondence in 1945, reported in February 1952 that thousands of Florentines protested in print and on the streets of "the City of Flowers" over modern architecture being constructed in front of the Ponte Vecchio, the only surviving bridge after the war.[39] "Human Beehives like great barracks" and "overgrown bird cages" were some of the names the Florentines gave these skyscrapers. Obstructing the Florentine landscape with a modern aesthetic was deemed an act of disrespect to the historic town. Cortesi wrote that, in an effort to stop any future developments, the people of Florence reached out to Mayor La Pira for assistance, who responded that he "would see what he could do."[40] When one walks through Florence today, it appears that the protesters received at least part of their wish. La Pira's passion for preserving Florentine culture was especially prevalent during the rejuvenation in Italian tourism during the 1950s. In fact, La Pira became entangled in efforts to retain priceless Renaissance artwork that he believed belonged to Florence.

The famed *La Muta* by Raphael, a prized piece of Florentine art originally owned by the Medici family, had been, up until World War II, shuffling back and forth between Urbino, Raphael's birthplace, and Florence. The artwork, like much of Europe's art at the time, had to be hidden from Nazi confiscation; this portrait of the eighteenth-century Florentine beauty Maddalena Strozzi was in Florence when the war broke out in 1940. After the war ended, the walled city of Urbino, located 115 miles east of Florence, requested that the painting be returned. One of the most circulated papers in the American South, the *Fort Worth Star-Telegram* in Texas, covered the deliberations in their piece "Urbino vs Florence - Dispute Over Famed Work Of Raphael May Be Ended," in which La Pira argued that "the clause preventing any work of art of the Medici family leaving Florence was still operative."[41]

La Pira felt that now and in the future, as in the past, work belonging to or commissioned by the Medici family belonged in Florence.

Urbino was certainly not going to give up the fight over their hometown artist, arguing that Italy had been an established single state since 1861, not a combination of republics and city-states as in the time of the Medici, adding that any contracts limiting the painting's movement during that time would now be null and void. The two cities, unable to come to an agreement on their own, had to reach out for assistance. It took a ministerial decree to finally have the portrait returned to Urbino. The *Fort Worth Star-Telegram* divulged that, in one last attempt, La Pira "offered in exchange another portrait by Raphael, of Cardinal Bibbiena, but the curator in Urbino [was] still unwilling to give up the masterpiece."[42] The battle was over and, as of today, *La Muta* hangs in the museum in the Galleria Nazionale delle Marche, Palazzo Ducale di Urbino. To La Pira, preserving culture was akin to protecting Florentine ideals.

Everyone is entitled to "a job, a house and music"

Two years before the end of World War II, in July of 1943, La Pira, along with members of Italian Catholic Action (a group formed to encourage Catholic influence in society), drafted the economic policy *Il Codice di Camaldoli* (The Code of Camaldoli). The code was named after the

Benedictine monastery Camaldoli, where the ideas were conceived.[43] Other influential Italians involved with the final draft of the code included future prime ministers Aldo Moro and Giulio Andreotti, jurist Giuseppe Capogrossi, activist Angela Gotelli, and philologist and literary critic Vittore Branca.

The Camaldoli code was based on the Belgian model of Malines of 1927 and curated by anti-fascist Catholic intellectuals. It emphasized the importance of the "dignity of the person, equality of individual rights, common good, functions of the state, primary destination of resources, distributive justice and social solidarity." The code specified that "to order economic life it is necessary to add to the law of justice the law of charity," designating that a public or private organization assist a member of society who is less fortunate through donations of food or housing. However, charity cannot be solely for the poor. Even if an individual has rightfully acquired all their basic necessities, other forms of charity could be of use.[44] La Pira believed that giving selflessly was crucial to uniting communities and, when implemented as a foundational principle of the government, would build trust between constituents and those leading them.

The Christian Democrats adopted the code as an economic guideline. Mayor La Pira, on multiple occasions, applied its policies in assisting the homeless and factory workers who were threatened with layoffs.

Everyone is entitled to "a job, a house and music,"[45] La Pira announced in 1953, around the time he was fighting for the rights of workers of the Pignone factory. The

Florentine factory, named after a village that once sat on the bank of the Arno, had a downturn in textile demand, forcing the stockholders to stop the plant's operation and institute an immediate closure. Franco Mariotti, the administrator of Società di Navigazione Italo-Americana (Italian-American Shipping Company), a synthetic textiles firm operating out of Milan, blamed the closure on competition from American products in the Italian market due to the Marshall Plan. His company had purchased Pignone in 1946 in an effort to exploit Pignone's expertise in frame manufacturing.[46]

For fear of unemployment, twelve hundred factory workers took matters into their own hands and "occupied the plant in effort to prevent it from being closed," as reported by the New York Catholic newspaper *Brooklyn Tablet* on December 12, 1953.[47] To prove to the workers that others besides the Communist Party were vigorously working on their behalf, La Pira, with help from local merchants, had food, water, and other supplies brought to strikers in the factory. The devout La Pira attended Mass with the workers in the factory courtyard and "talked strategy with the communist-dominated union committee," according to the *Time Magazine* article "The Saint & The Unemployed."[48]

The *Tablet* ran the headline "Reveals Pope Had Role In Sit-Down Strike," and reported that La Pira sent an urgent letter to Pope Pius XII and received a "papal blessing on his campaign" to save the factory. The pope responded to La Pira through the Vatican Secretary of State, Monsignor Giovanni B. Montini, who in 1963 would become Pope

Paul VI. The message was that he "hoped that both management and civil authorities who had already done much to remedy the situation" would push beyond their limits so the employees could "enjoy the indispensable security that comes from continuous employment."[49]

As the strike continued, La Pira appeared to be at a loss as to how to resolve the matter. Advice from his close friend, Minister of the Interior Amintore Fanfani, gave La Pira what he needed. Fanfani suggested he reach out to Enrico Mattei of the recently formed Ente Nazionale Idrocarburi (National Hydrocarbons Authority).

La Pira reportedly told Mattei he was confident that ENI would purchase Pignone because "the Holy Spirit" had told him so. Mattei responded that he had the "utmost respect for the Holy Spirit," but that he couldn't purchase the factory for the primary reason that ENI dealt in oil and not textiles.[50] La Pira's perseverance and compelling arguments evidently convinced Mattei, however, for, along with the help of government orders, it wasn't long before the workers of Pignone were celebrating ENI's taking them into their fold and reintroducing the firm to the world market as Nuovo Pignone.

There were mixed opinions in America regarding how the Pignone predicament was handled. In an op-ed entitled "A Lesson from Abroad" published in the *Troy [NY] Times Record* on December 24, 1953, La Pira and the Italian government's actions were called "socialist schemes." The "progressive steps" taken by La Pira and the Italian government to save the factory inspired the author to write a warning to the United States. The demand for a guaranteed wage and the nationalization of Pignone was "a signal to stop and think, it could happen here."[51] "It" was a communist upheaval of republican ideals backed by a socialist agenda. Anti-communist sentiment was at an all-time high in the United States and colored much of the reporting on Europe during that time.

On the side which championed La Pira's decisive action, correspondent Marquis W. Childs in the *St. Louis Post-Dispatch* described La Pira as "dedicated to raising living standards for the lowest level," and credited him with keeping "several hundred Florentines from being out of work and onto the relief rolls." The headline for Childs's piece, published April 25, 1954, however, was somewhat alarming: "Real Danger of Communist Hold on Italy is Difficult to Evaluate"—an ominous thought during the height of McCarthyism.[52]

During this time, some of the best writers in America were covering politics in Europe, revealing the deep connection the two continents still shared and a belief that what was happening there could happen here. For more than thirty-six years, Marquis W. Childs was a foreign correspondent, chief Washington correspondent, and a columnist for the *St. Louis Post-Dispatch*, winning a Pulitzer for distinguished commentary during 1969. Childs wrote of the growing power of the Communist Party in Italy, summarizing that Italians in government positions believed Americans worried unnecessarily over growing communist support. Childs felt differently and believed the Italians were taking an apathetic approach in anticipating that once their economy rebounded, communist support would decline.[53]

In 1954, the Christian Democrats were said to be the single largest party in Italy's coalition government, but any attempt at progress was hindered by the parties on the far right. There were some politicians in Italy, Childs explained, who were scaring the "wits out of the right wingers . . . who [feared] them more than they [did] the Communists." One of those politicians was the "Outstanding" Mayor Giorgio La Pira, a man who exuded great "warmth and a hearty humor that have helped to make him an almost legendary figure."[54]

Revealing La Pira's regular acts of charity, Childs references an incident that took place during a political rally La Pira presided over, where Prime Minister Alcide de Gasperi was to speak. La Pira asked if, before any talk of politics, he could take up a collection for the poor. De Gasperi was put on the spot when La Pira turned to him to say that he "was sure the Premier would want to contribute 10,000 lire (about $16). Somewhat shamefacedly, de Gasperi produced 5000 lire, which he said was all the money he had with him."[55]

It was only a year after saving the blue-collar jobs in Pignone that La Pira intervened to help save, in the interest of "public order," one hundred jobs at the Fonderia Delle Cure (the Cure Foundry) after the owners had filed for bankruptcy.[56] The foundry specialized in the production of pig iron; the hot metal, obtained from blast furnaces, contains around 4 percent carbon along with other natural impurities.

"Italian Mayor Seizes Foundry, Turns Firm Over To Workers" was how the *Baltimore Evening Sun* captured the story on February 18, 1955, proclaiming that Mayor La

Pira had once again found himself at the center of a swirling storm of protest. Unsurprisingly, the article described La Pira as "small, quiet, absent-minded," adding that "he [spent] most of his time in a monastery."[57]

In defense of his social activism, La Pira was said to have announced, "The Le Cure Foundry will be a real stronghold of resistance to injustice and we shall see who wins."[58] However, his methods were not championed by all, and a piece in *Time Magazine* claimed, "The legality of Giorgio's requisition was, to put it mildly, highly dubious. As justification for it, Lawyer La Pira cited an 1865 law empowering requisition in case of disaster, and a similar clause in the present constitution—ignoring the fact that the intent in both cases was for the national government to take over, not a municipality."[59]

As in the case of Pignone, La Pira "hurried" off to Rome to seek assistance from government officials after learning that the foundry's owners, unhappy with the steps La Pira had taken to occupy the foundry, were possibly going to pursue the matter in court. Fortunately, through an undisclosed buyer, new orders of pig iron were placed. In the end, La Pira was able to turn over the foundry's operation to a co-operative workers group and raise enough funds to "set up a monthly indemnity to pay off the owners."[60]

The *Indiana [PA] Gazette* reported that "the soft-spoken little mayor" didn't disclose the source of the new business and that there was speculation that the Italian government, "embarrassed by La Pira's action at a time it [was] trying to find foreign capital," had to step in to assist with the foundry's recovery.[61]

ITALIAN MAYOR UNDER FIRE OVER PLANT[62]
February 18, 1955 - *Indiana Gazette*, Indiana, PA

STORM OF PROTEST GATHERS OVER
SEIZURE OF ITALIAN PLANT[63]
February 18, 1955 - *Bridgeport Telegram*, Bridgeport, CT

MAYOR OF FLORENCE TAKES OVER MILL,
STIRS AN UPROAR[64]
February 18, 1955 - *Asbury Park Press*, Asbury Park, NJ

STORM RAGES OVER ITALIAN MAYOR
WHO SEIZED PLANT[65]
February 18, 1955 - *Progress-Index*, Petersburg, VA

PLANT SEIZURE BY MAYOR IN ITALY
IS PROTESTED[66]
February 19, 1955 - *St. Joseph News-Press*, St. Joseph, MO

Plenty of papers criticized his actions, including his hometown newspaper *La Nazione*, which asked, "How can we approve what he has done without also approving anarchy?" The communist newspaper *L'Unita* praised his actions as a "courageous application of principles."[67] Such public acclaim from a communist newspaper was likely the impetus for some critics in the United States to begin focusing more intently on La Pira's behavior.

Attorney James C. Ingebretsen was one such critic. Ingebretsen was a member of the Los Angeles Chamber of Commerce, and for a time served as the chamber's representative in Washington, DC. In 1945, Ingebretsen was appointed a member of the board of LA harbor commissioners, despite strong disapproval from union leaders who were concerned over his lack of experience dealing with issues within the port.[68] Later in his career, he became president of the ultra-conservative organization Spiritual Mobilization, which received the majority of its donations from large corporations. The vehemently anticommunist founder of Spiritual Mobilization, Reverend James W. Fifield Jr., believed that the "blessings of capitalism come from God," and that to uphold the core principles of Christianity, one must live and work within a free-market economy.[69]

In "Pause For Reflection," published on June 26, 1955, in the *Monitor* newspaper based in McAllen, Texas, Ingebretsen had more questions than information about the mode by which La Pira requisitioned the foundry. Although he believed that the mayor meant well, he was "puzzled" by La Pira's logic.[70]

The article reads as though Ingebretsen believed that the workers were not competent enough to run the foundry on their own. Seemingly concerned, Ingebretsen questioned "whether La Pira gave the workmen the foundry to show them that, even though they owned it, they would have to work, and someone would have to manage things with a fair amount of wisdom if cashable paychecks were ready for them on pay day—or whether he gave the plant to them as a reward for their striking."[71]

Ingebretsen accused La Pira of "trying to govern Florence according to the rule of St. Francis," although in his opinion, "St. Francis would have difficulty seeing how the action of the mayor fits into the conception of solving all problems with Christian love."[72] In acting by his Christian morals, La Pira seemed to conflate church and state, according to Ingebretsen, or at minimum resemble socialist behavior.

Mayor saves plant, drums up business[73]

However he could manage it, the ever-astute La Pira would continue to save plants and factories around the Tuscan region, including Galileo, a manufacturer of optical instruments, in 1959. The company was eventually nationalized and, 156 years after its formation, is still in operation today.[74]

In the 1950s and 60s, communism was portrayed as the biggest threat to the American way of life, not only because of the possibility of nuclear war, but because it threatened the core principles that hold American democracy together. Even though Americans feared the philosophy of communism, labor unions were in their heyday in the mid fifties, with over 35 percent of the labor force in the United States unionized.[75] Senator Joe McCarthy of Wisconsin didn't help matters much, stirring up a frenzy after he accused a number of US government officials and members of public and private organizations of communist activity. During this period, the United States more than tripled its defense spending in anticipation of elevated conflict during the Cold War.

It seems that in 1951, when La Pira unseated the incumbent communist mayor Mario Fabiani, the United States finally took notice of the unassuming Sicilian, with the press hyper-focusing on La Pira's ability to gain a following within largely communist-run northern Italy. Critics merely exposed the enigma that was La Pira, instead of bringing him down: his actions were equalizing due to his altruistic nature, not a communist disposition.

Throughout La Pira's political career, correspondents, reporters, and politicians had conflicting opinions regarding his relationship with communism. The *New York Times* reported that certain critics went as far as calling La Pira "sinister" and claiming, "his boundless goodwill extends even to the communist."[76] La Pira's "sinister" side was defined in relationship to the 30 percent increase in the communist vote in the 1960 municipal elections and to Florentine debt reaching a record high, as reported by the *Times*.

In "Philosophy of Communism," a series of diplomatic essays published in 1952, La Pira wrote: "Communism was a theological system of culture. . . . Christianity is by its very structure exclusive. . . . Because of that, it eliminates all other theologies." La Pira asked Christians to "meditate" and make their choice between communism and Christianity.[77]

Considering that the United States had a vested interest in defeating the "Red Scare" in every region of the world, any meeting or correspondence La Pira had with Russians was regularly reported.

The red bear of Moscow beckons

During a twelve-day goodwill visit to the United States in 1955, Italy's Prime Minister Mario Scelba met with President Eisenhower and Secretary of State John Foster Dulles. It was expected, as reported in the *New York Times* on March 28, 1955, that the three-day meeting in Washington would be consumed with talks over the burgeoning communist allegiance in Italy.[78] A prospect of more concern for Prime Minister Scelba was the possibility of a ten-year economic recovery program in partnership with the United States. Scelba bartered for a better trade balance and hinted that, for the sake of Italy's economy, he would turn to Russia if need be. He threatened that if he didn't formalize his ideal agreement with the United States, "The red bear of Moscow beckons."[79]

On November 14, 1955, the *Corpus Christi Caller-Times* published a piece written by journalist Houston Harte, a close friend to Lyndon B. Johnson and the founder of the Texas-based marketing company Harte-Hanks Media. The article covered La Pira in a way that became a recurring trope. Harte wrote that "The Northern section of Italy [was] a communist stronghold; Giorgio La Pira, the mayor of Florence, [was] the only non-communist mayor in the whole of Northern Italy."[80]

During this time, the United States Information Agency, known as the United States Information Service (USIS) in Italy, was created with the primary purpose of promoting public diplomacy and "to prevent both the Fascist and Communist from taking over any government within."[81] Numerous American politicians condemned USIS for wasting taxpayer dollars, but Harte, in the closing paragraph of his piece, defended the program. He wrote that if the nation can spend "$34 Billion a year on national defense, it doesn't seem too much to gamble about a third of 1 percent on something that might hold the line for freedom and democracy."[82]

L'Informatore del Vermont New Hampshire e Maine was an Italian semi-monthly based out of White River Junction, Vermont,[83] and was considered to be the only democratic newspaper in the state.[84] Printed in both Italian and English, the paper circulated throughout New Hampshire, Vermont, and Maine until dissolving in 1959. On November 26, 1955, *L'Informatore* published, in Italian, a report of the visit of a Russian delegation to Florence consisting of the Vice President of the Council of Ministers of the Soviet Union, Vladimir Kucherenko; and the USSR Ambassador to Rome, Aleksandr Bogomolov. After the delegation visited numerous public works in Florence, they were received at the Palazzo Vecchio, where "mayor Prof. Giorgio La Pira, who was ill, addressed them with words of greeting." Kucherenko, after having recalled that Mayor La Pira was invited to visit Russia, said: "We are perfectly convinced that our visit to Italy will serve to strengthen the friendship between the Italians and Soviets and contribute to strengthening peace for all peoples."[85] La Pira, accompanied by a friend, journalist Vittorio Citterich, would take the Russians up on their invitation in 1959.

Improve their lot without bartering their liberty

The *Daily Times* of Salisbury, Maryland, published a story under the headline "It Would Have Been Easy" on April 4, 1955. This time, correspondent Arnaldo Cortesi posed a question to Prime Minister Scelba before he departed the United States. Cortesi inquired, considering that Italy was "believed to have a larger proportion of communists in its population than any other country in Europe, even Russia itself," what did Scelba think about La Pira's anti-communist successes? Cortesi highlighted that "La Pira [had] started a grassfire in the field of anti-communist action" and "as a practicing Christian, the Mayor [had] taken it upon himself to befriend the downtrodden instead of letting them go to the local communist agitators by default." Cortesi referenced La Pira's declaration that the people of Italy "can improve their lot without bartering their liberty," a statement that led many, throughout the Tuscan region, to abandon their support of the Communist Party in favor of La Pira and the Christian Democrats. It was Cortesi's belief that "La Pira's idea could have been applied generations ago in Asia, where cynical colonialism drove millions of Asiatics into the beckoning arms of disgusting tyrants." He quoted General MacArthur's comment that "Asia [was] ripe for revolution, the communists merely have taken advantage of it, the Christian nations [had] turned their backs on it"—a remark that now appears to foreshadow the Vietnam War.[86]

It was also around this time that Cortesi, in the *New York Times*, brought to light the condition of the slums that

Florence was attempting to clean up. He divulged that the more than four thousand homeless people living in makeshift lodging were being cared for at the expense of the city, and that the "slum quarter of Santa Croce" was treating two thousand children for tuberculosis. These scenes, according to Cortesi, would go unnoticed by the multitudes of tourists visiting the vast collection of art the city had to offer, as this image of poverty was inconsistent with American romanticisms of Italy.[87]

The city of Florence, Cortesi wrote, was "going deep in the red," as Mayor La Pira worked tirelessly to relieve the suffering of the "poorer folk," which in turn increased the city's "so-called social expenses," resulting in the municipality running at a loss.[88]

The deficit was at $3,000,000 in 1955, Cortesi's article revealed, with taxes reported by some at an already "maximum bearable level." A private bill by Tuscan deputies was presented to the Italian Chamber of Deputies that would hopefully relieve Florence of its worrisome financial troubles. The municipality would "float" a loan of $50,000,000 from the government.[89]

Santa Croce and San Frediano, "fine residential quarters in medieval times," possessed antique buildings of historical and artistic merit, but were by then considered "slums." With support from the loan, "La Pira proposed the idea of transferring the inhabitants of the two slums to new homes that will be built on low lying ground along the River Arno." In addition, the funds would go toward increasing the water supply, building new schools, revamping the antiquated sewage systems, and constructing new municipal offices.[90]

Moreover, La Pira intended to have the fourteenth-century Palazzo Vecchio retain only the mayor's office and to make the rest of the complex into a museum. Cortesi speculated a few months ahead of the 1956 elections that efforts to improve the city at the "eleventh hour" had the ability to stimulate La Pira's chances for re-election.[91]

In 1956, with fascism and communism on the rise throughout the world, the United States was keeping an intent eye on Italy's upcoming elections. It was reported by Robert E. Jackson in the *Sacramento Bee* that La Pira had "tremendous appeal," winning "the hearts of Florentines by living a monk-like existence, spreading most of his salary to the poor, while confiscating luxurious, but uninhabited villas for the homeless." It was believed that La Pira was the "only obstacle to the Communist," reported Jackson.[92]

While trying to secure new democratic voters, the communists were on their best behavior during the run-up to the 1956 election. Meanwhile, the "fascists were yearning for the empire heyday of Mussolini [and] . . . clashed with police in Rome."[93]

La Pira and the Christian Democrats were keeping the Communist Party at bay, thanks in part to La Pira's growing reputation, the influence of Catholic Action, and an information-gathering technique adopted from the communists. In order to gain additional support in rural and poorer regions of Italy, Amintore Fanfani, the Christian Democrats' campaign strategist, recruited and trained hundreds of youths from areas in the south in an effort to understand the party's strengths and weaknesses.[94] The youths worked in their own communities gathering information on public viewpoints of social wants and needs. The technique paid off, except for one serious drawback.

Even though the Christian Democrats accumulated as many votes as their opponents combined, the revision of an election law—which the Christian Democrats had implemented—resulted in the party losing some seats and, consequently, majority control in many important cities.[95]

The *St. Louis Dispatch* covered the 1956 elections with great enthusiasm and detailed the specifics of the updated law in "Pro-West Bloc Loses Full Grip On Rome, Right Holds Balance - Communist Slip in Major Cities But New Law Puts Fascist, Monarchist in Strategic Position."[96] Formerly, the party with the most votes in a city obtained two-thirds of the seats on that city council. The Christian Democrats revised the law so that, in cities with a population of over ten thousand, each party was granted an equal opportunity by allotting seats on a percentage basis. However, "this attempt to satisfy the minor parties cost the center group full control."[97] The Christian Democrats' attempt to even out the playing field had backfired on them.

The US government, conceivably nervous about how the new law might affect the outcome of the upcoming Italian election, had discussed the policy change during a Committee on Appropriations hearing in 1956. Leaders in Congress remarked on how "under a revised election law . . . amendments . . . [had] removed much of the advantage . . . to the center parties in contests for communal council," therefore making it "more favorable to the opposition parties." In regional and local Italian governments in 1956, there were over seven thousand communal council seats and seventy-nine provincial council seats up for grabs.[98]

ELECTORAL LAWS AID ITALY REDS[99]
May 26, 1956 - *Republican and Herald*, Pottsville, PA

ITALY'S CHRISTIAN DEMOCRATS
LOSE CONTROL IN KEY CITIES[100]
May 26, 1956 - *Journal Times*, Racine, WI

IN ITALY: CHRISTIAN DEMOCRATS
GAIN AT REDS' EXPENSE[101]
May 29, 1956 - *Press Democrat*, Santa Rosa, CA

Mayor Monk Elected Again Thru A Quirk

The US government was most likely thrilled to learn that, "through a quirk" in an Italian election law, La Pira once again was elected mayor in 1956.[102] His opponent, socialist Raffaello Ramat, was a professor of Italian literature at the University of Florence and in 1941 had founded the anti-fascist magazine *Argomenti*.

The mayor of Florence was chosen by the city council in 1956 when, after the votes were tallied, both candidates had each received thirty-seven votes. The "quirk" in the law was that in the event of a tie, the older man gets the job.[103] It's reported that after the Christian Democrats remembered the law, they yelled out ecstatically, knowing that La Pira was one year older than Ramat. It wasn't until

1993 that the law was changed, and in 1995 the first mayor elected by popular vote was University of Florence professor Mario Primicerio.

The headlines were varied and sensational, but the single Associated Press release that spawned them once again focused on La Pira's ascetic life: "Controversial Giorgio La Pira has been re-elected mayor of Florence by a margin of one year." That's right. The bird-loving Christian Democrat, sometimes called "the Modern St. Francis," was named to the office by the city council because he was 52, one year older than his opponent.[104]

WINS MAYOR POST BECAUSE OF AGE[105]
August 4, 1956 - *Times Standard*, Eureka, CA

FLORENCE MAYOR WINS REELECTION BECAUSE OF AGE[106]
August 4, 1956 - *Boston Globe*, Boston, MA

ELECTED MAYOR BY A WHISKER[107]
August 4, 1956 – *Mt. Vernon Register-News*, Mt. Vernon, IL

LA PIRA ELECTED AGAIN - BY A YEAR[108]
August 5, 1956 - *Philadelphia Inquirer*, Philadelphia, PA

CRUSADER REELECTED[109]
August 5, 1956 – *Dayton Daily News*, Dayton, OH

MAYOR MONK ELECTED AGAIN THRU A QUIRK[110]
August 8, 1956 - *Times-Advocate*, Escondido, CA

La Pira's political achievements and pursuits went unreported for a period in the American press, with the exception of a couple of human-interest pieces. The American press didn't report that La Pira had to resign from the office of mayor in June 1957 because of the lack of a majority vote on the city budget, nor that in the interim period, a prefect had appointed a commissioner to administer the city of Florence.[111] The coverage didn't pick up again until his campaign for and subsequent reelection to the office of mayor in 1961.

Fascism Tide Surges in Italy - Libel Suits Cited[112]

Under pressure to form a new government in Florence, La Pira, "the most controversial figure in Italian Politics," was elected mayor for the third time in 1961. Anna Brady of the *Baltimore Sun* wrote that the "Italy Regime [was in a] New Peril" due to the Florence coalition adding pressure on the government. Brady reported that an "agreement was finally reached three and half months after elections had failed to give a majority in Florence to the center parties."[113]

La Pira's newly formed government caused a melee between a few communist-left and rightist party members during demonstrations in Florence, resulting in several injuries.[114] George Armstrong described in the *Scranton [PA] Times-Tribune*, on March 22, 1961, how Mayor Giorgio La Pira was physically threatened after he called the neo-fascists "'an evil weed' and promised that he would 'uproot it' from Florence."[115] In retaliation, the Neo-Fascist

Party filed a libel suit against the mayor, exclaiming that they would make a "political enemy" out of La Pira.[116]

The war of words turned to mob intimidation one day while La Pira was attending Mass. A group of neo-fascists, while attending a meeting in a nearby hotel, got word of La Pira's whereabouts and "marched to the church door armed with lead pipes, clubs and bicycle chains" all the while "singing Fascist hymns and looking for trouble." Luckily for La Pira, a few friends notified him of the threat and were able to sneak him out safely through a side door.[117]

According to the Italian constitution, it was illegal to form or pay tribute to the fascist party, but the law was never really enforced. La Pira sent a message to President Giovanni Gronchi demanding that he use his "Presidential powers to have the neo-fascist party outlawed." The Christian Democrats added their thoughts in the liberal press, saying, "'It would be a good idea if we all smiled a little less indulgent and paid more heed . . .' to Fascist youth activities."[118]

Florence and the world

La Pira's new term was once again reflected in published accounts of Italian-Russian diplomatic affairs. During an International Space Symposium held in Florence, La Pira is shown in a *New York Daily News* photo from April 13, 1961, congratulating Russian scientist and diplomat Anatoly Blagonravov on the success of the first manned space flight.[119]

Beginning in October 1962, during the Cuban Missile Crisis, the United States' space program cooperated with Blagonravov, who went on to work alongside NASA's Dr. Hugh Dryden as part of the United Nations Committee on the Peaceful Uses of Outer Space.

Nuclear disarmament became yet another exhausting battle for La Pira, who showed no qualms in writing to world leaders, hoping his efforts would sway them away from the warpath. The response to one of La Pira's letters to Khrushchev was featured in the *Dayton [OH] Journal Herald* on November 6, 1961. Khrushchev had made public his response to the letter, in which La Pira pleaded with the Soviet leader to "end nuclear testing." Khrushchev wrote that "if the West continues its present policies there is danger of atomic war." The Soviet Union had felt justified in their recent testing, pointing out that they still trailed the West in the number of nuclear trials and explosions.[120] In a few short paragraphs the article detailed the strain between the Soviet Union and United States, which ultimately led to the Cuban Missile Crisis a year later.

The fourth Mediterranean gathering organized by La Pira "to debate the question of minorities everywhere" took place in Florence in June 1964 and was covered by Robert C. Doty, foreign correspondent and press spokesman for the United Nations Food and Agriculture Organization. Reporting for the *New York Times*, Doty summarily described La Pira as "a small, ebullient man who [sat] in a large office built for a Medici Pope and [thought] about Florence and the world."[121]

The colloquy was attended by an estimated 140 unofficial delegates from many different countries. Doty noted that La Pira was "convinced that the Mediterranean world [was] and should be the center of Western civilization, that Italy is the focus of the Mediterranean world and that Florence, seedbed of the Renaissance, is the heart of Italy."[122]

Doty, in a passing interview with La Pira in between sessions, reported that La Pira "spoke with deep conviction and rushing enthusiasm of the necessity and inevitability of reconciliation in the 'family of Abraham'—the Jewish, Christian and Moslem peoples of the Mediterranean." La Pira finished the interview by expressing that "the problem of the world is piloting," going on to say, "President Kennedy understood it well—the world has become so small, we are all so close—if you have courageous piloting you can change the situation."[123] As one of the only articles wherein La Pira references Kennedy, Doty's piece clearly expresses La Pira's great admiration for the recently assassinated president.

In the run-up to the 1965 mayoral election, La Pira, according to the *Abilene Reporter-News* published in Texas, was said to be frequently "backed by the Communists," and due to his "left leaning views" had lost support from within his own party.[124] This election concluded with La Pira second to his opponent from fourteen years earlier, Italian communist Mario Fabiani.

In sessions that ran through the night, the city council elected Fabiani as mayor of Florence and in doing so made Florence the "largest city in Italy with a communist mayor." However, the *Abilene Reporter-News* reported that, unable to give the city a government, Fabiani immediately resigned. It was noted in the newspaper that the city council had been vigorously working to form a government "ever since the council was elected last year and former Mayor Giorgio La Pira lost his majority."[125]

Giorgio La Pira had presided over the office of mayor from July 5, 1951, to June 27, 1957, and from March 7, 1961, to February 15, 1965. The defeat in 1965 resulted in La Pira never seeking public office again. He shifted his focus, time, and energy to peace in Southeast Asia and beyond. Nonetheless, La Pira had generated waves during his time as mayor of the city of Florence, waves that continued to reverberate so profoundly that he became world renowned for his championing of peace and human dignity causes.

3

"Unite the Cities to Unite the Nations"

At the time of the "Great Arrival," Italians made up more than 10 percent of the foreign-born population in the United States. During a time when complexities surrounded their newly unified country and earthquakes and disease plagued the southern region, nearly four million Italians chose to leave Italy and immigrate to the United States between 1880 and 1920.[126]

Although 20 to 50 percent would return home (the *ritornati*, "returned"), the ones that did stay in the United States kept in close contact with those back home.[127] The American press seized this opportunity to capitalize on new readership by reporting near-daily minutiae coming out of even the tiniest of Italian villages. The two countries' bond was further strengthened, this time politically, when Italian Foreign Minister Carlo Sforza signed the North Atlantic Treaty on April 4, 1949, in Washington, DC, joining the

NATO alliance in an effort to stabilize Italy's economy and support its aspiration to be a key player in the world.[128]

While members of the newly formed alliance were getting to know one another, NATO rolled out buses called the "Caravan of Peace" to illustrate its purpose to the people of Italy.[129] The travelling exhibition made stops in Turin, Milan, Genoa, Bologna, Venice, Florence, Rome, Bari, and Naples. The buses distributed posters and leaflets explaining how NATO worked and were equipped with a movie projector to further detail NATO's ambitions. The caravan was a tremendous success: more than 1.5 million visitors attended the exhibitions, spurring the extension of the program in some variation into the 1970s.[130]

Throughout the 1950s, the United States fell into a love affair with Italian culture, the US Catholic Church had its highest number of Mass attendees, and the fear of communism was at its pinnacle. It was the perfect trifecta for a man like Giorgio La Pira to come into the consciousness of the American public.

His many visits with American politicians, institutions, and citizens led to many letters, telegrams, and newspaper articles describing a mutual respect garnered with the humble mayor of Florence. The government officials La Pira received from the United States during his time as mayor usually had a political agenda, or at least a moment during their vacation where some sort of politicking would take place. La Pira was well versed in Italian history, and he used that knowledge to point out on multiple occasions the connection or influence his beloved city of Florence had with the rest of the world. La Pira's voice extended across the Atlantic to the smallest corners of the United States. He went from a local figure to a globalized personage even before his first visit to American shores, which came in 1964.

Tied by a Florentine knot

It was La Pira's philosophy that cities throughout the world, no matter how big or small, should have a role in the building and preserving of peace within a nation, and ultimately the world. In a speech given at an assembly of the International Red Cross Association, he said: "All cities . . . historic or recent, artistic or otherwise are all alike. They unanimously claim their inviolable right to exist: no one has the right, for whatever reason, to destroy them."[131] He made his ultimate goal clear: "We must unite the cities to unite the nations."[132]

Six years after the war, the United States was still in the process of promoting a "better understanding of the United States among the peoples of the world and [strengthening] cooperative international relations," according to the initiative set forth in the United States Information and Educational Exchange Act of 1948.[133]

One of the first politicians from the United States to visit La Pira during his first term as mayor was Sicilian-born New York City mayor Vincent Impellitteri, along with his wife Elizabeth. Impellitteri had not been back to his birthplace in over fifty years, and the *New York Times* reported that "he regarded himself as an example to Italian people of how a poor immigrant could rise through the democratic processes to become mayor of the world's largest city."[134]

Impellitteri's thirty-five-day goodwill tour of Italy and Israel was praised by President Truman and the Secretary of State for Public Affairs, who wrote in a letter to Impellitteri that the trip would "be helpful for furthering friendly relations between Italy and the United States."[135] The trip was covered extensively in the *New York Times* from the day he flew out of Idlewild directly to Rome, to his return out of Naples on the Italian liner *Vulcania*.[136] The *Philadelphia Inquirer* reported on October 8, 1951, that the mayor and his wife "were welcomed by Mayor Giorgio La Pira and a crowd of cheering Florentines."[137]

Impellitteri, who had a "reputation for honesty," was born in the northern Sicilian town of Isnello;[138] La Pira was born almost directly south in the town of Pozzallo. When Impellitteri met La Pira, he said in the Sicilian dialect, "*cca semu tutte Sicilian*," "Here we are all Sicilians."[139] One can only imagine the pure joy the two humble Sicilian natives must have felt when meeting each other for the first time.

At a ceremony in 1954 honoring the five hundredth birthday of Florentine-born explorer Amerigo Vespucci (the man for whom America was named), La Pira described the relationship between Florence and America as "tied by a Florentine knot," as quoted by Richard Ehrman in the *Newport News [VA] Daily Press*.[140] La Pira added that "Americans owe something more to Florence," pointing out that a Florentine navigator, Giovanni da Verrazzano, "discovered an island on which now stands the city of New York."[141] The previous year, La Pira had, in celebration of the three hundredth anniversary of the European discovery of the island of New York, cabled warm greetings to his friend Mayor Impellitteri and the people of New York.[142]

ITALY CITY FETES MAN
FOR WHOM AMERICAN NAMED[143]
June 14, 1954 - *Daily Press*, Newport News, VA

FLORENCE NOTES VESPUCCI DAY[144]
June 14, 1954 - *Billings Gazette*, Billings, MT

HOME TOWNERS HONOR
NAMESAKE OF AMERICAS[145]
June 14, 1954 - *Albuquerque Journal*, Albuquerque, NM

ITALY CELEBRATES VESPUCCI'S BIRTH[146]
June 14, 1954 - *Austin American*, Austin, TX

The Saint

In his first trip abroad after the war, former President Harry S. Truman and his wife Bess celebrated their thirty-seventh wedding anniversary with a tour of Europe. In a series of articles for the *Miami Herald* in 1956, Truman wrote fondly of his time in Italy. The president remarked, "We've been fed too well by so many wonderful people" and that Florence "is a great center of attraction for the ladies of the family, who enjoy themselves the most because they can buy more here than in any other place in Italy."[147]

A little less than a decade before, in March 1947, Truman had drafted the Truman Doctrine, which outlined basic foreign policy in an effort to contain the spread of communism in Europe. The doctrine was, in part, a pledge to support any country that held back revolutionary communism and successfully limited the scope of the Soviet Union, a foreign policy that would guide US diplomacy for the next forty years.

Ironically, Truman, nicknamed "the old campaigner," arrived in Florence on election day in May 1956.[148] In his book *Off the Record: The Private Papers of Harry S. Truman,* he wrote that he spent his time in Florence visiting "famous places," perhaps underscoring that he believed Americans had a broad knowledge of what these "famous places" were.[149] It was reported elsewhere, for example in the *Bristol [TN] Herald Courier,* that Truman and his entourage visited the Uffizi Gallery and Academy of Fine Arts. Most galleries in Italy are closed on Mondays, the *Courier* reported, but after learning who the visitor was, they "hastily" opened their doors for the former president.[150]

On May 29, 1956, a headline from the *Boston Globe* read, "Truman Congratulates Italian Mayor on Win." The paper announced that La Pira, who "led the center coalition to local victory," was congratulated by Truman on his "hard fought victory . . . despite a strong communist-socialist bid for power."[151]

When Truman and his party departed, La Pira saw them off at the train station and wished them Godspeed as they headed to Venice.[152] Truman, in his book, wrote briefly of his time with La Pira: "The mayor had just been re-elected and of course he was very happy. . . . He is a remarkable man and lives a private life that causes him to be called . . . 'the Saint.'"[153]

TRUMAN CONGRATULATES ITALIAN MAYOR ON WIN[154]
May 29, 1956 - *Boston Globe*, Boston, MA

ITALIAN MAYOR GIVEN PRAISE BY TRUMAN[155]
May 30, 1956 - *Chattanooga Daily Times*, Chattanooga, TN

TRUMAN LAUDS ITALIAN VICTOR[156]
May 30, 1956 - *Pittsburgh Post-Gazette*, Pittsburgh, PA

Since I am mayor, I should meet the mayor of Florence!

In October 1962, Hugh A. Wayne, mayor of San Mateo, California, was missing his family, who were traveling throughout Europe. So he hopped on a plane to meet up with his loved ones in Rome. They then headed north to Florence, where the family toured the wineries of the Tuscan countryside and viewed the work of the Renaissance masters in the Uffizi Gallery and Galleria dell'Accademia.

Wayne's daughter Suzy, who was 22 at the time, remembers the day her father suddenly announced, "Since I am mayor, I should meet the mayor of Florence!" According to Suzy, her father was very much a diplomat and, like La Pira, believed in the benefits of the sister city program. San Mateo itself established a sister city partnership with Toyonaka, Japan, the following year.

After a few phone calls and the requisite bureaucratic red tape, Mayor Wayne had his meeting set with Mayor La Pira. Never one to miss a photo-op, explains Suzy, her father had arranged a local photographer to document the event. The meeting took place at City Hall inside Palazzo Vecchio, and along with the photographer, Mayor Wayne also brought with him a copy of Dante's *The Divine Comedy.*

Suzy recalls the day with great fondness. "There was plenty of handshaking," she said in an interview conducted for this book, commenting that La Pira "was very kind, constantly smiling and courtly."

Even though Wayne spoke no Italian and, as Suzy witnessed, La Pira not much English, the two mayors did their best during the forty-five-minute meeting to get to know each other.

Back home in California, the *San Mateo Times* published a photo from the meeting illustrating how Mayor Wayne received an explanation of "some of the original manuscript reproductions in a new edition of Dante's *The Divine Comedy.*"[157] In the photo, La Pira is gesturing to the book as Mayor Wayne looks on smiling. The photo, says Suzy, was displayed proudly in her dad's office until his retirement.

Just a few days after the meeting, Wayne, due to the escalation of the Cuban Missile Crisis, felt it necessary to cut his trip short and rush back home to San Mateo.

Far-left Roman Catholic Mayor

In 1963, La Pira, backed by a unanimous vote of the city council, declared Burmese-born U Thant an honorary citizen of Florence. It was an honor that seems deserving of more than the few sentences of press coverage it got, considering that Thant, the third elected Secretary-General of the United Nations, was an instrumental mediator in the peaceful solution to the Cuban Missile Crisis. On July 13, 1963, the *Democrat and Chronicle* out of Rochester, New York, quoted Mayor La Pira saying that U Thant was being honored for "happy actions of peace undertaken by him in the most dramatic moments of . . . the Cuban and Congo Crisis."[158]

But not all dignitaries who arrived in Florence would be as warmly received by the masses for one reason or another, as in the case of Mohammad Reza Pahlavi, better known as the Shah of Iran. The shah implemented a statewide government program in 1963 called the White Revolution, which included granting women voting rights, increasing infrastructure development, and reducing illiteracy. Some critics viewed the reforms as an effort to westernize Iran.[159]

When the shah arrived in Florence in 1964, local Iranian students posted propaganda and protested in the streets, chanting "down with the Shah."[160] The *Arizona Daily Star* ran the headline "Shah's Visit to Spa Draws Protest," detailing that students had accused him of "indulging in la dolce vita." The shah was visiting the Tuscan hillside spa Montecatini to experience the "bitter water" cure, which was speculated to work wonders for matters of the liver. Students were primarily angry about the limited amount of money they were able to receive from home after the shah implemented financial austerity.[161]

Local Florentine police quickly shut down the demonstration and arrested several of the protesters. It was reported in the *Arizona Daily Star* that the "far-left Roman Catholic mayor Giorgio La Pira, nicknamed 'The Saint,' who had been missing at the civic welcome of the Shah, pleaded with the police to release the students."[162]

A "prominent Florentine"—Marquis Emilio Pucci, fashion designer, politician, and one-time confidant of Mussolini's daughter Edda—criticized La Pira for not receiving their imperial guest. As a recently elected member of parliament, Italian Liberal Party member Pucci sent off an urgent "formal request to the Roman government to instruct Mayor La Pira how to receive an imperial guest in the ancient city of grand dukes."[163] However, there are no newspaper reports of how the government responded, giving the impression that the demand was simply dismissed.

New Frontiers

The first Conference of the Mayors of the World's Capitals took place in Florence in 1955. La Pira invited mayors from around the world, even from a few communist countries, to discuss his plan for "peace of the cities of the entire world, which makes a pact of brotherhood at the very basis of the life of nations." It was also during this time that La Pira began promoting the idea of a sister city program between Florence and other important cities around the world.

Nine years after these initial plans were set in place, La Pira visited the United States for the first time in early October 1964 to formally launch the Florence-Philadelphia sister city program, cities which he referred to as "two great centers of culture."[164] The *Philadelphia Daily News* on October 10, 1964, cheekily announced La Pira's arrival as being not by the ships of Columbus, the "Pinta, Nina, or Santa Maria," but simply by flight.[165]

La Pira had a busy schedule: the Columbus Day parade, a concert by the Philadelphia Orchestra at the Academy of Music, and a Sons of Italy banquet, where he was formally introduced by Philadelphia Mayor James H. J. Tate.[166]

At Independence Square, La Pira shared speaking honors with Mayor Tate, who hoped that the sister city program would act as a "real approach to understanding between the peoples of the world." La Pira addressed the crowd in Italian while being translated by the "grand recording secretary of the Sons of Italy." As quoted in the October 12, 1964, edition of the *Philadelphia Inquirer*, La Pira stated that Philadelphia was the "heart and pillar of the United States." He added, profoundly, "Our first thoughts and prayers are offered to the forefathers of the American nation . . . and to all the Presidents of the United States. To them, providence has entrusted a mandate: the mandate of the new frontiers: a mandate which is delivered day by day, for the life, freedom and happiness of the American people and, as a consequence, of all the peoples of the world."[167]

During the day's ceremony, La Pira presented a bouquet of flowers to the Columbus Day Queen and placed a wreath on the statue of Christopher Columbus in Philadelphia's Fairmount Park.

Giorgio La Pira (third from left) at the tenth annual Columbus Day Parade in Philadelphia.
© 1964 Robert Halvey, *Catholic Standard & Times*, Archdiocese of Philadelphia.

Professor Mario Primicerio, who accompanied La Pira on his visit to the United States, recalled that their schedule was packed with many meetings. After Philadelphia, they went on to New York City where La Pira met Secretary-General U Thant, Cardinal Francis J. Spellman of New York, New York City Mayor Robert F. Wagner Jr., US Ambassador to the United Nations Adlai Stevenson, peace activists Peter and Cora Weiss, President of the World

Jewish Congress Nahum Goldman, and NASA Director Dr. J. DeFrance.[168]

Primicerio recollected that La Pira was in a meeting at the State Department with the US Ambassador to the Soviet Union, Llewellyn Thompson, when "at that very moment . . . Khrushchev's fall was announced"[169] after a Kremlin coup, ending his ten-year reign.

The tour of America continued to Louisville, Kentucky, where La Pira met with American Trappist monk Thomas Merton at Gethsemani Monastery. The two men held a mutual admiration and respect for one another. Merton described La Pira as "ebulliently Christian, but a very good head too."[170] The meeting was the start of a deep and enduring friendship, rooted in faith and a commitment to peace.

La Pira established many long-lasting relationships with the prominent and influential people he met during his initial visit to the United States, and some went on to play significant roles in his life during times of great conflict.

5th Army Vets visited G.I. Graves in Italy

On October 7, 1952, two Midwest papers, the *St. Joseph Gazette*[171] out of Missouri and the *Des Moines Register*[172] in Iowa, covered a story of US veterans of the Fifth Army returning to Italy to pay respects to their fallen compatriots. An estimated 1.5 million Italian-Americans served in World War II, the largest percentage of any minority in the US armed forces. The heroic Fifth Army, under the command of US Lieutenant General Mark Clark, were the first American force to invade mainland Europe on September 9, 1943, and the first to liberate a European capital—Rome—from fascist control.

La Pira paid tribute to soldiers from the United States who helped liberate the whole of Italy from fascist dictator Benito Mussolini and honored the veterans with a reception after the soldiers had visited the American Florence Cemetery and Memorial in the town of Tavarnuzze.[173] Located 7.5 miles south of Florence, the cemetery is the resting place of soldiers who died during the capture of Rome in 1944 and the fighting in the Apennine Mountains in early May 1945.

Some stories covered the lighter side of the American soldiers returning to Italy, as well as the solemn moments. "He's Out of One Army, Ready for Another" was plastered on the cover of the *Minneapolis Star Tribune* on April 15, 1953, highlighting the amusing story of a recently naturalized American citizen who found himself in a conundrum after traveling back to Italy to get married.[174] The couple, groom Alfonso Mazzarella and bride Graziella, married in Rome and were honeymooning in Florence when the police detained the young man, who had the American and Italian draft boards after him.

Mazzarella was arrested for evading compulsory military service.[175] Under an Italian law at the time, men were required to enlist for mandatory military service. Mazzarella "pleaded that he had to get back to his adopted home in New York to report to his draft board by April 27, but that did not soften police hearts."[176] In 1953, the Italian law stated that any Italian man who became a citizen of another country was still subject to mandatory Italian military service.

Whoever solved Mazzarella's problem is not mentioned, only that the Italian army drafted Alfonso, then twenty minutes later gave him an honorable discharge and handed him back his American passport.[177] The *Montpelier [VT] Evening Argus* revealed that the next morning, Giorgio La Pira, sent his personal car to the newlyweds' boarding house to pick them up as his luncheon guests, perhaps providing a hint as to who helped their cause.[178] In a photo published in the *Hartford [CT] Courant*, the newlyweds look hypnotized as La Pira talks in his typical fashion, punctuating his words with his hands.[179]

So, when the news was announced that two stars of the silver screen were planning their nuptials in a town filled with Renaissance beauty during a heated local election, it scrolled across newspaper headlines. Hollywood was probably jealous that they didn't think of the story first.

Prim Florence Mayor

Italian cinema was in its golden age in the mid-1950s with directors such as Federico Fellini, Vittorio De Sica, and Roberto Rossellini mixing realism and fantasy into a whole new genre. Stars Marcello Mastroianni, Sophia Loren, and Monica Vitti displayed style and elegance that Americans tried to emulate.

Real-life romance took center stage in May 1956 after Swedish film star Anita Ekberg and British actor Anthony Steel announced that their wedding would take place in Florence. Ekberg had recently been in Rome filming *War and Peace*, and four years later would become a top commodity in Italian cinema after her appearance in Fellini's *La Dolce Vita*.

A plethora of newspapers reported on the highly anticipated wedding, which had the misfortune of being scheduled during "thick . . . Italian political campaign" for the upcoming local election.[180] In addition to the mayoral race and the near riots caused by Ekberg's adoring fans, there was a question of who was going to officiate the ceremony.

Mayor La Pira was the obvious choice to preside over the ceremony, but he was dealing with more pressing concerns regarding his re-election campaign, and furthermore "[did] not approve of civil marriages," as the *Times Record* in Troy, New York, put it. Considering that Anthony Steel had been divorced, and Florence was a strong Roman Catholic city, La Pira didn't want to "risk the loss of votes."[181] Because La Pira refused to marry them and Ekberg's residency in Florence wasn't official, the wedding plans were delayed.[182]

The "prim Florence Mayor Giorgio La Pira, a saint-like person who talks to birds and lives in a monastery," as described by the *Arizona Republic*, "had intervened only a few hours before the marriage to stop the plans."[183] At that point, according to the *Spokane [WA] Spokesman-Review*, the couple decided it was best to head off on a prenuptial visit to Lake Cuomo to wait for the religious and legal strings delaying their wedding to untangle.[184]

The *Times Record* recorded that "La Pira [had shunned] the wedding to an antechamber after lesser city authorities had arranged for the use of the great hall," which fit five hundred people. A city official announced that "the solemn hall . . . was not a suitable place for a wedding," as it was unfurnished and bare. It was understood that the sole reason for the supposed switch was that La Pira faced "a tough struggle against the communist opposition" in the upcoming election and needed to conceal this marriage.[185]

With the rise of the Italian Communist Party, journalists from the States had been covering the election ferociously. The event was a campaign roadblock because La Pira, a supporter of the arts, was uninterested in the marriage of a famous film star on the basis of his religious beliefs, yet wished to maintain the American-Italian cultural exchange. At such a poignant moment in the election, the promotion of the wedding was a potential threat to his incumbency and spurred a conflict between two of La Pira's strongest political motivators, art and religion.

Eventually, after Steel's Italian lawyer spent a week cutting through the official bureaucratic paperwork, the couple returned to Florence and were married in front of a noisy "jam-packed crowd" in the antechamber of Palazzo Vecchio. City official Menotti Riccioli performed the ceremony, although he had to stop more than once because the couple and witnesses could not hear over the screaming throngs of fans in attendance.[186] Despite the earnestness with which they fought to have the wedding they wanted, the couple did not live so happily ever after, and divorced three years later.

Another couple, who would celebrate their fourteenth wedding anniversary later that year, made a trip to Florence on May 8, 1961. The *Hartford Courant* briefly covered the royal visit of Queen Elizabeth and Prince Philip and featured a photo of La Pira walking onto a platform to make a speech as the royals stood before a Florentine banner, looking on. La Pira and other Florentine city administrators warmly greeted Queen Elizabeth and Prince Philip, whom some Italians had nicknamed "Pippo." Mayor Giorgio La Pira formally welcomed the queen and her husband into the city "as trumpeters dressed as 14th century heralds, blared out a salute." The *Hartford Courant* finished by declaring that the couple received "a reception unlike any given the queen thus far."[187]

Despite this coverage of the visit, very little detail about the event accompanied the large photo printed in many American papers, perhaps illustrating that the image of the queen, dressed in the latest fashion, and La Pira, wearing his mayoral sash and delivering a welcome speech, told the story itself.

Star of Solidarity

During the 1950s and 1960s, Florence was the epicenter of fashion in Italy. The Sala Bianca in the fifteenth-century Pitti Palace was said to be the birthplace of ready-to-wear fashion. La Pira passionately supported the arts and, as mayor, recognized Florence's newfound influence on the world and celebrated the individuals who contributed to it.

No area appeared off limits to La Pira or to the American appetite for coverage. In the "Women" section of the Los Angeles Times, a letter from Giorgio La Pira was published on July 23, 1956, wherein he wrote to *Times* fashion editor Fay Hammond, congratulating her on her "contribution toward the success of Italian fashion." The previous year the Italian government had bestowed upon Hammond the "Star of Solidarity" for her "service" to their "country through fashion reporting." In the letter, La Pira wrote that Florence would be awarding Hammond its coat of arms and the "Golden Lily," which would be presented to her while she was reporting on the upcoming fashion season in the Sala Bianca of the Pitti Palace. Hammond once referred to the Sala Bianca as "Crystal-lit Sumptuousness."[188]

La Pira was again drawn into the world of fashion in July 1964, when American teenager Suzanne Lechner's dream came true when she won a contest sponsored by Hess's Department Store. Ann Brewster, in the *Morning Call* of Allentown, Pennsylvania, wrote of Miss Lechner's win in a piece titled "Cinderella Story Is Full of Thrills For Hess's Teen-Trip-of-a-Lifetime Winner!"[189] Lechner had won an eight-day trip to Italy to attend the opening of fashion week in Rome and Florence, and she herself walked the runway of the Pitti Palace in a gown designed by Wanda Roveda.

Brewster wrote that "Suzanne delighted the mayor of Florence, Prof. Giorgio La Pira . . . when she told him about her trip and when she presented to him tokens of appreciation from Allentown's mayor and Max Hess, president of Hess Department Store—so delighted him that he gave her gifts for them and herself." In the photo that accompanied the article, Lechner is all smiles as La Pira, with his right hand on his chest, appears entirely sincere as he talks with the young American.[190]

Italian Symphony

In a dedication made to the city of Florence, the Minneapolis Symphony Orchestra sent recordings of their April 4, 1952, concert to Florence to be played on Italian radio. The orchestra had recorded two pieces: Respighi's suite *The Birds*, which seemed fitting since La Pira kept two birds in his office, and Mendelssohn's "Italian symphony," *Symphony No. 4*.[191]

Two months after the April concert, Minneapolis Mayor Eric Hoyer received a message from La Pira in response. In a radiogram to Mayor Hoyer, which was translated and printed in the *Minneapolis Star Tribune* on June 22, 1952, La Pira wrote that he was "grateful and proud of being the recipient of the artistic homage sent from the illustrious city of Minneapolis."[192] La Pira continued that he, in return, would dedicate to Mayor Hoyer a "great symphonic-choral Rossini concert, directed by Antonino Votto on the 29th of June, commemorating the seventh centenary of the [Basilica of the] Most Holy Annunciation."[193] His correspondence concluded with his hope that there would be "further artistic collaboration between Minneapolis and Florence."[194]

Musical dedications continued to play back and forth between Florence and the United States for years, including La Pira's tribute to the Denver Symphony Orchestra during a special 1962 concert at Palazzo Vecchio, which was featured in the *Austin American*. La Pira was extending his thanks after the Denver orchestra had referred to "Florence as the cradle of the Italian renaissance" the previous year.[195] Almost exactly a year later in 1963, the University of Tennessee Singers were introduced in front of the Uffizi Gallery by Mayor La Pira. The *Greeneville Sun* in Tennessee reported that "Dr. J. E. Arnold dean of extension, presented to Mayor Giorgio La Pira, the special greetings of Tennessee's Governor Frank Clement and the famed proclamation to which the state's executive and the legislature named the singers, 'Tennessee's musical ambassadors to Italy.'" To show his appreciation, "Mayor La Pira met personally with the 50-voice choral group and was their host at an elaborate reception that followed the program."[196]

Florentines Fight Art Loan to U.S.[197]

Florentine citizens were proud of their fine collection of art, to such an extent that in October 1956, a *diffida* was filed in their name by artist Enrico Sacchetti against

Mayor La Pira and the superintendent of Florence's public art galleries, Professor Filippo Rossi. This appeal, a kind of cease and desist, was made in an attempt to keep forty paintings from being shipped to the United States, reported the *Hartford Courant*.[198] The collection, scheduled to be displayed in the National Museum in Washington and the Metropolitan Museum of Art in New York, included Botticelli's *Birth of Venus* and Raphael's *Sitting Madonna*.

Concerned, Mayor La Pira warned the superintendent of museums to suspend preparations to send the masterpieces to America. In a letter to Superintendent Rossi, La Pira expressed the possible "repercussions on public-order" if the masterpieces were to be shipped.[199] The other immense issue of concern, as reported in the *Hartford Courant*, was the sinking of the Italian ocean liner *Andrea Doria* three months prior.

The *diffida* emphasized that the sinking "shows that priceless cargo could not be adequately insured against loss."[200] Bernard Berenson, American expat and preeminent authority on Renaissance art, was outspoken in his objection to shipping the art to America. La Pira, in an effort to explain the situation, sent a telegram to the *New York Times* to express that the "true motives of the controversy . . . were purely artistic," rather than political.[201] The Italian Supreme Council on Art wound up opposing the idea of sending any Renaissance art to be exhibited in New York or Washington, explaining that the risk of losing the priceless pieces outweighed any benefit of cultural relations.

Students Sound Theme of Democracy

Three years after his election as mayor in 1951, reports of La Pira's success in fighting communism found their way to the rural towns of middle America. La Pira's words and actions had affected a high school senior so profoundly that the student mentioned La Pira in his graduation speech. The headline "Students Sound Theme of Democracy" was published in the *Galesburg [IL] Register-Mail* on June 4, 1954, and featured speeches from three students graduating from Galesburg High School.[202]

"The Future, a Challenge for Democracy" was the theme of Julian Bockserman's speech. Bockserman told the story of an Italian man, Giorgio La Pira. "This man represents the story of Democracy," he told members of his graduating class. He continued, stating that La Pira "is working to rid Italy of communism." "In order to do this, La Pira feels that he must first rid Italy of the things Communism thrives on—doubt, hunger, ignorance and greed," Bockserman concluded.[203]

You have to pray with the world map on the bedside

Perhaps La Pira's most notable contribution to the world was his humanity and the many ways in which he shared it. La Pira, who had been quoted saying, "You have to pray with the world map on the bedside," was very much aware of the world's injustices, and at times reached far beyond the borders of Florence in his efforts to right wrongs and make the world a better place.[204]

Over the span of three years, two telegrams were published that showed La Pira's humanitarian concerns. One was sent in an attempt to halt the execution of a San Quentin (California) inmate, Caryl Whittier Chessman. The second focused on the execution of a Spanish communist.

Caryl Whittier Chessman had become an "international crime celebrity" after he was sentenced to death in a California court for robbery, kidnapping, and rape. During his time in San Quentin and Folsom Prisons, Chessman had written four novels, one a 1954 international best seller titled *Cell 2455, Death Row: A Condemned Man's Own Story*.[205] La Pira's cable to California Governor Edmund Brown was published in the *Journal Times* of Racine, Wisconsin, and emphasized that "any last-minute act of mercy by the governor would be 'a great judicial, human, Christian and political act' of immense service to future civilizations."[206] Unfortunately for La Pira and other protesters around the world, the plea for clemency fell on deaf ears. Chessman was the first American executed for a non-lethal crime; he died on May 2, 1960, twelve years after his sentencing.

The *Fort Worth Star-Telegram* published an excerpt from a fiery telegram La Pira sent to military dictator Francisco Franco in April 1963, in which he condemned the Spanish general for the execution of communist Julian Grimau Garcia, saying, "You have stained with blood the noble land of Spain."[207] Garcia was a member of the Spanish Communist Party during the Spanish Civil War, as well as chief "criminal investigator," hunting down supporters of Franco.[208] During the three-year war, Garcia oversaw the execution of dozens of Franco loyalists.

After Franco defeated the Second Spanish Republic, Garcia fled to France, residing there for several years. He eventually snuck back across the border into Spain in an attempt to reestablish the Spanish Communist Party. Not long after his return, Garcia was captured by Madrid police, tried, and found guilty of the executions he oversaw twenty-five years earlier. La Pira's strong condemnation of Franco was reported in the *Star-Telegram* on April 22, 1963, which cited his prayer: "May the Lord forgive this crime which created such profound sorrow. . . . May this sorrow accelerate the irresistible movement of freedom of the Spanish people against a tyranny that stamps with blood its final decline."[209]

By the 1960s, La Pira had made his mark in the international arena as a pioneer in building transnational relationships through the arts, honorable conduct in diplomatic affairs, and strengthening Florentine economic statecraft. La Pira believed that leaders of municipal bureaucracies should not be stifled by the scope and geography of their position. His strategy as a leader was to transform Florence from a cultural center to a globalized political center. American journalists and newspapers had been following his journey as a political figure for a decade, while his transcontinental efforts to unite the cities, and ultimately, the nations, had remained the same.

4

The Holy Mayor

There is no denying that Giorgio La Pira was a man of faith, hope, and charity. In 1925, at the tender age of 21, he took the name of Fra Raimondo as a part of the Third Order of Saint Dominic. He expressed his role as a layperson in a letter to his Aunt Settimia Occhipinti in April 1931: "There is no doubt that the Lord instilled the desire for priestly grace into my soul. He wants me to continue my lay apparel so that my work will be more fecund in the secular world that is far from him."[210]

The press frequently compared La Pira to the fifteenth-century Dominican friar Girolamo Savonarola because both advocated for social justice and resided in cells in the Convent of San Marco. Further, Savonarola was considered a model of reformed Catholicism by leaders of the Christian Democratic Party.[211] A statue of the Dominican friar currently stands beside the tomb of La Pira inside San Marco.

Politics is a commitment
to humanity and holiness

In early 1950, La Pira organized the International Congress for Peace and Christian Civilization, stating, "Politics is a commitment to humanity and holiness."[212] Maurizio Renzini, founder of the Italian Thomas Merton Society, quoted Romans 4:18 in his essay "Thomas Merton and Giorgio La Pira: A Friendship for Peace": "Hoping against hope, he believed that he would become 'the father of many nations,' according to what was said, 'so numerous shall your descendants be.'" This verse, he believed, best summarized the "guiding principle for the human, spiritual and social action of Giorgio La Pira."[213]

It seems very appropriate then that during La Pira's first year as mayor, the city of Florence carried out an act of repentance for the death of Fra Girolamo Savonarola, who was unjustly hanged and burned for acts of heresy on May 23, 1498. The *Spokane Spokesman-Review* covered the beginning of the four-month-long commemoration on May 24, 1952, with the headline "Tributes Paid To Savonarola," wherein it was written that La Pira publicly apologized to the Convent of San Marco for the execution of Savonarola, while students placed white flowers on the spot in Piazza della Signoria where he was executed.[214] Presently, Savonarola is under consideration for beatification by the Catholic Church.[215]

La Pira, despite his own adherence to strict Catholic doctrine, appreciated gatherings where ideas, philosophies, and varying opinions could be discussed openly, without judgment. The first Conference for Peace and Christian Civilization was held in Florence in July 1952. At the request of the US State Department, Dr. Charles W. Lowry, rector at All Saints Episcopal Church of Chevy Chase, Maryland, attended the inaugural event and reported the proceedings for Religion News Service. The *Des Moines Tribune* published Dr. Lowry's account under the headline "Tells Parley of U.S. Link to Religion."[216]

Dr. Lowry described his disappointment over what little knowledge attendees had about how crucial religious life was in the United States, but he made sure to point out that Florence's mayor, the former "university professor, had defeated Communist forces in the election last year."[217] In his speech during the conference, Dr. Lowry announced, "It is this Christian link, this Christian foundation . . . which sparks and unites the United States in its leadership in the fight against Communism and all that it represents."[218] Dr. Lowry said that the resolution adopted by the conference "embodied much of the spirit of a declaration he proposed" as members sought a means for preserving the state of Christian civilization and peace in Italy.[219] Dr. Lowry considered the United States' long-standing heritage of Christian values as the defining factor keeping communism from invading the free markets of the US economy and American institutions.[220]

The second Conference for Peace and Christian Civilization was held on June 21, 1953. In very few words, the *Albuquerque Journal* summarized the conference: the overarching theme of the meeting was "prayer and poetry" and it was attended by representatives from thirty-nine

Western countries brought together by their nationally embedded Christian principles.[221] La Pira presided over the conference and greeted the representatives, including the recently appointed US Ambassador to Italy, Clare Boothe Luce, on whom the Italians had bestowed the label *la Signora*, the Lady.[222]

39 WESTERN COUNTRIES OPEN PEACE CONGRESS[223]
June 22, 1953 - *Albuquerque Journal*, Albuquerque, NM

2ND CULTURAL CONGRESS OPENS IN ITALIAN CITY[224]
June 22, 1953 - *Arizona Daily Star*, Tucson, AZ

PRAYER AND POETRY[225]
July 3, 1953 - *Catholic Advance*, Wichita, KS

Luce, in 1953, was the first woman appointed to a major ambassadorial post abroad and retained the position until 1957. Passionately anti-communist herself, the Roman Catholic ambassador regarded La Pira as a strong ally in upholding the key principles of American ambition. The pair corresponded quite frequently and established a warm personal rapport during Luce's years as ambassador.[226]

As reported in a study declassified and released on February 7, 2017, Luce had been involved in overseeing a secret CIA financial support program targeting centrist Italian bureaucracies with the purpose of diminishing the Italian Communist Party's hold on labor unions. The

Defense Department's historical study showed that between the late 1940s to the early 1960s, the United States sent $5 million in aid annually to Italy.[227]

Italian Red Hints at Vatican Offer[228]

Two separate reports in the *New York Times* on May 19 and 20, 1953, provided varying degrees of detail about a failed "religious truce" between the Vatican and the Soviet Union two years earlier. It was reported on May 19 that the Vatican, through an undisclosed "go-between," had contacted the Italian Communist Party in 1951 to declare that the Vatican would be inclined to drop their "policy of indiscriminate support of American initiatives," if the Soviet Union would "open up negotiations on religious questions and peace."[229]

However, the Vatican newspaper, *L'Osservatore Romano,* maintained that the "go-between" had approached the communists of his own accord. Furthermore, the newspaper reported that the unnamed liaison spoke with a communist senator purely regarding "the possibilities that he thought he could see on questions and situations of a religious character and not properly of peace." The leader of the Italian Communist Party, Palmiro Togliatti, suggested that the comment of "negotiations on religious questions and peace" was entirely "vague and generic" without substantiated means, and pressured the unnamed "go-between" to formally document the conversation and his ideas. Togliatti characterized the man who contacted the communist party as a former "Christian Democratic party deputy" who was currently mayor of a "great Italian city."[230]

Such a letter detailing the deputy-turned-mayor's ideas was eventually written and sent to Togliatti, and later published in *L'Osservatore*. As reported on May 20, 1953, Togliatti had found the proposition, now revealed to be authored by one Giorgio La Pira, credible enough to present it "in the highest quarters," presumably meaning to Kremlin leader Joseph Stalin. The Kremlin replied that they were pleased with anyone who was seeking to "join the Partisans of Peace," a statement that could "hardly be taken seriously," according to La Pira.[231]

The May 20 *New York Times* article also reported that during a speech in northern Italy, Togliatti divulged Moscow's initial enthusiasm over the possibility of negotiations, but blamed failed attempts at such negotiations on the Vatican for refusing to withdraw its wholesale support of American ambitions. The sole reason "peace did not reign between the Roman Catholic Church and communism," said Togliatti, was due to Vatican loyalty to American endeavors in combating communism. According to *L'Osservatore Romano*, the issue was dropped relatively quickly and La Pira "never spoke of it again, neither to one side or to the other."[232]

The articles appear to suggest that La Pira considered himself a "peace feeler" and, without authorization from the Vatican, had overestimated his capacity as mayor of Florence to bring forth open dialogue between Russia and the Vatican. But then again, the two articles were a bit convoluted in their detailing of events, dramatically "uncovering" the identity of La Pira as the man behind the negotiations in the manner of an investigator solving a deep mystery.

In the end, neither article clearly establishes whether La Pira had tried to improve Vatican-Soviet relations, initially without permission, by taking advantage of an opportunity to pursue a religious peace deal or if the Vatican undermined public statements made about negotiations with the Kremlin so as to not upset their American alliance.

Florence Mayor Inspires a Word[233]

On March 28, 1955, Arnaldo Cortesi of the *New York Times* reported that a new word had been composed which hadn't appeared in any dictionary before: *Lapirismo!*[234] The freshly coined word was Italian slang that defined a Christian spiritual movement advocating measures against poverty and unemployment.

Cortesi detailed, much like his *New York Times* colleague Anne O'Hare McCormick had a few years earlier, La Pira's "unshakable faith" and his belief that "Christian Love" could solve all of man's dilemmas, even communism. There was only one way to rid Italy and the world of communism, according to La Pira, and that was to show that elected leaders are the guardians of the "humble . . . and lower class." La Pira strongly believed that it was Christians who must advocate for what some Italians referred to at the time as the "inferior class."[235]

During an interview that took place in La Pira's "magnificent" office in the Palazzo Vecchio, two canaries in a cage distracted him, as he would frequently turn to admire them with great affection. La Pira discussed his inability to sleep most nights while lying in his bed in the cell of San Marco, knowing that there were homeless families without a roof over their heads. "There is no denying his warmth and sincerity of his love for his fellow man," Cortesi observed.[236]

Further, La Pira elaborated on a recommendation he had sent to the municipal council suggesting they send a bottle of milk to each prisoner in the city jails. The idea was met with a callous response from critics on the right, replying that the prisoners' diets had plenty of protein. Somewhat annoyed, La Pira responded, "What have proteins to do with it. . . . The milk I wanted to send was full of love."[237]

Cortesi concluded by describing La Pira's great joy in two recent accomplishments: a "satellite city" which had been built on the outskirts of Florence for homeless workers, and the fact that the factories he had commandeered were still in full operation, providing "full employment."[238] La Pira was adamant about protecting the rights and livelihoods of those he served as mayor, even those he indirectly served as a religious leader.

In June 1956, during the fifth Conference for Peace and Christian Civilization, La Pira pleaded for the release of Cardinal Stefan Wyszyński of Poland. Stalin had imprisoned the cardinal and other clergy in 1953 under the suspicion of "anti-government activity."[239] The *Plain Speaker,* headquartered in Hazleton, Pennsylvania, covered the conference and printed that the "Leading Roman

Catholic layman," Mayor Giorgio La Pira, "blamed" Stalin directly for the detention.[240] The paper said that "the Ascetic" mayor believed the trials were immoral and unfair, and furthermore, were "decisively influenced by a man whose immense iniquity has now been officially admitted by the leaders of those (Communist) states."[241]

RELEASE OF CHURCHMAN SOUGHT[242]
June 23, 1956 - *Minneapolis Star*, Minneapolis, MN

SUGGESTS RUSSIA FREE CLERGY JAILED
UNDER STALIN REGIME[243]
June 23, 1956 - *North Adams Transcript*, North Adams, MA

Cardinal Wyszyński, along with fellow clergy, was released in 1956 during Polish October, the period of Poland's battle for political reforms and efforts to overcome Stalinism. The *Wichita Catholic Advance* published on February 1, 1957, that La Pira received a letter of thanks from Wyszyński in response to a cable that he had sent upon the cardinal's release. The cardinal declared that "mankind will enjoy happier days once differences between people will have been solved . . . not through the use of force, but through justice and love."[244]

After Florence, there is only heaven

The *Tablet*, a Catholic newspaper published by the Diocese of Brooklyn, New York, celebrated La Pira's unwavering quest to lift up the downtrodden. Not long after the 1956

Conference for Peace and Christian Civilization, Fr. James I. Tucek wrote that Giorgio La Pira's "moving spirit" and "almost poetic flair" should be emulated by the Catholic world. Fr. Tucek detailed La Pira's devotion to his faith and his intense desire for social justice, which caused some to characterize him as "a St. Francis Assisi in politics."[245]

La Pira considered America's contemplative religious orders commendable and important to the structure of US Christian institutions, more so than the US military capacity, bolstered as it was by their possession of the atomic bomb.[246] La Pira recognized that devotion to prayer rather than direct action cultivates a population focused on thought and religious meaning, a testament to the American foundation built upon a constitution that examines parallels between Christian values and freedom. In his mind, America was taking the first step in believing that thought breeds action.

The Tucek article provided a short biography, covering La Pira's birth in Sicily, his time as a University of Florence professor of law, and his success as mayor. One of La Pira's first acts as mayor, Fr. Tucek points out, was his donation of one million lire to a local orphanage. When asked about the large sum, La Pira responded, "This is one of the best financial investments we could make. A million to the . . . orphanage means a billion to the city."[247]

A few of La Pira's many good deeds for the poor were mentioned, such as his requisitioning of abandoned private villas for the homeless. Critics argued that housing should only be supplied after a natural disaster, like a flood or earthquake, causing La Pira to counter, "For the homeless who has no roof over his head, the earthquake has already happened."[248]

At the time of the article's publication in June 1956, La Pira was 52 years of age and had spent thirty of those years in Florence, a city he absolutely loved. Fr. Tucek wrote that La Pira, as mayor, felt he was the "father of the city" and had expressed that "after Florence, there is only heaven."[249]

In 1950, the *Cronache Sociali* (*Social Chronicles*) published two essays by La Pira, "L'attesa della povera gente" ("The expectation of the poor people") and "La difesa della povera gente" ("The defense of the poor people"), in which he describes his opposition to the absolute dominance of neoclassical economic laws.[250] Attuned to the destitute conditions of lower-class individuals, La Pira had remained steadfast against viewing the poor as economic capital or as a burden throughout his political career.

Two Masses of the Poor Are Offered Each Sunday

A "[sudden] element of joy and youth . . . like a ray of sun" is how Mayor La Pira is described in the *Brooklyn Tablet* on May 18, 1957, as he entered Santi Apostoli, knelt at the altar, and plunged himself into prayer. Hymns were sung, the Gospel was read, and a prayer to the poor written by La Pira was recited. In the city of Florence, Italy, this "Director of Unusual Charity" held two Masses for the poor every Sunday, one for women and one for men.[251]

The *Tablet*, courtesy of Religion News Service, beautifully detailed the event, averring that La Pira, "the bachelor . . . who lives in a monastery cell," was believed by many to be the father of the poor for his consistent acts of charity and piety. The *Tablet* was the first to mention the welfare group the St. Procolo Society, which La Pira founded in 1934 and which donated the baskets of bread to be handed out the day of the Mass. After Father Spinelli had blessed the bread, using the recommended "Latin formula," La Pira was handed the book and read it again in Italian, "because nobody would understand the Latin," he said.[252]

La Pira stood in front of the altar and talked to the women about local events. He spoke passionately of the "virtues and missions" of saints, leading the congregation in a prayer for those who had died that week. He spoke of charity above all and how "Florentine missionaries carried the Christian message to the ends of the world."[253]

The last few sentences of the article summed up La Pira's demeanor that particular Sunday. He possessed "eloquent gestures . . . burning sincerity and a radiant face," and his warm words seemed to "cast a spell over" everyone in attendance. With "renewed peace and comfort in their hearts," the women exited the church, and received the donated loaves of freshly baked bread.[254]

The author does not remark on anything unusual about La Pira's charity. Was it unusual to find a mayor so principally involved in the daily feeding, housing, and spiritual uplifting of the poor inhabitants of his city? It appears that it was, to some.

Italian Mystic Mayor Gives Russians Religion[255]

Nikita Khrushchev's anti-religion campaign was in its infancy when La Pira, who at the time was a member of the Italian Parliament, visited the Soviet Union in the fall of 1959, a first for a "prominent member of the Italian government."[256] The visit was seen as significant for La Pira, who was said to have had a great influence on former Italian Prime Minister Amintore Fanfani's views on foreign policy. Fanfani was in a bid to lead the Christian Democratic "party machine" in the upcoming October elections, as reported by the *New York Times*.[257]

George Armstrong, reporting for the *Boston Globe*, relays the finer points of the "Mystic Mayor's" visit behind the Iron Curtain in 1959. La Pira, sometimes called "the Pint-Sized Savonarola," had just returned from the shrine of Our Lady of Fatima in Portugal when he received an invitation from the editor of the Soviet Union newspaper *Pravda* (*Justice*).[258] He accepted the invitation and was accompanied by his good friend Vittorio Citterich, editor-in-chief of the *Giornale del Mattino*, a Florentine newspaper that focused chiefly on international politics.

Focusing on La Pira's ascetic life, like most correspondents at the time, Armstrong provided a vibrant biography of the "Saintly Mayor" who lived as a guest in the Convent of San Marco, where Fra Angelico had painted the cells with "priceless frescos."[259] He, again like many other journalists, emphasized the poignant moments when La Pira would venture out into the cold only to return home without his coat after passing it off to someone less fortunate.

La Pira reckoned the invitation from *Pravda* was an "invocation from the Virgin Mary." He believed that he was going to Moscow on a "mandate from the Madonna," explaining that "one of the prophecies of the Madonna at Fatima was 'that Russia will be converted to Christian ways and will know peace.'" The urgent necessity to be in Moscow on the Feast of the Assumption was evident to La Pira; the experience of his holy pilgrimage inspired him to act promptly and head east. The only problem was that he had but a week to procure a visa for travel.[260]

Since La Pira was not a "communist bigwig," it could have taken several months for him to obtain a visa. Armstrong wrote: "The diminutive, bouncy La Pira bounded into the Russian Embassy in Rome and explained that he needed to get to Moscow in time for the Assumption." The Russian consul was said to have greeted La Pira bluntly, stating, "As you can imagine, professor, I am a Marxist." La Pira quickly responded, "Oh I know. . . . I'm going to Moscow purposely to pray for you."[261] The manner in which the conversation continued is unreported, only that the visa was granted and that La Pira arrived in Moscow, as he said he would, on the eve of the Assumption.

Armstrong pointed out that packed in his suitcase, which contained shirts and socks made by nuns and one extra suit, La Pira included calling cards of "Madonna and the Annunciation," the famous painting by Fra Angelico. On the back of the card was a prayer composed by La Pira and translated into Russian. Armstrong states he handed the cards out to "every comrade and commissar he met." On his first full day in Moscow, La Pira, along with a disconcerted Kremlin official of cultural affairs, attended Mass at the Catholic Church of St. Louis.[262]

In the middle of La Pira's visit, *Pravda*, possibly seizing an opportunity to influence him, published an article on the progress of the Soviet Union's agriculture industry and the progress they had made "in their struggle against religion." La Pira replied by sending a scolding letter to the paper, exclaiming that the Soviet Union "should stay out of religious matters. . . . Let the believers believe and encourage the non-believers to respect the religion of others."[263]

After Moscow, an undeterred La Pira headed off to one of Florence's sister cities, Kiev, to hand out more of his calling cards. Back in Florence, the Florentines figured that La Pira would only return home once all of his cards had been given out. Knowing his custom, they also suggested the high probability of him returning without his extra suit, predicting that he would give it away to someone in need.[264]

In the West, La Pira's reputation was spreading far and wide within the US Catholic community. *Catholic Boy* and *Catholic Miss* magazines, in January 1962, awarded a young student of St. Boniface School in Sioux City, Iowa, second prize for her article on Mayor Giorgio La Pira. The *Sioux City Journal* did not publish the young student's essay but stated that Miss Joanne Kelly had beat out twelve hundred readers who had written on the topic of the Florentine mayor.[265]

The United States, with its flourishing Christian communities and abhorrence of communism, became a haven for Catholicism, deepening the schism between these two polarized ideals. Pope Paul VI was the first pope to visit the United States, on October 4, 1965, and a few weeks later, according to the *San Francisco Examiner* on October 28, 1965, was "seriously examining" plans to travel to the Eastern Bloc for the one thousandth anniversary of Poland's conversion to Christianity.[266]

The *Examiner* reported that "former mayor of Florence, Giorgio La Pira, an extreme left wing Catholic [was] in Poland making the final arrangements for the papal visit," adding that the Vatican was denying the reports of an upcoming visit.[267] The trip never materialized, with some blaming the potential lack of security for the millions of Polish Catholics who would attend. Others assumed political unrest associated with the Polish-German border after World War II would erupt. Whatever the reason, Pope Paul VI never set foot in Poland.

La Pira's loyalty to his faith acted as his compass throughout his personal and political life. He used the Christian religion not as a weapon, but as a tool in an effort to help others be better, do better, and ignite social change. La Pira sought to redirect and redefine how Christian morals were embedded in Italian culture, society, and politics. His unwavering religious devotion appeared to inspire others both at home in Italy and in the small towns of middle America. For the most part, it was throughout this time before 1965 that La Pira's faith and devotion garnered praise and respect from the American press.

The coverage of his endeavors by American journalists helped to spread his idea that true merciful action was preached in the church but founded in altruism.

Christianity was an active influence on La Pira's diplomatic strategy, not because he approached politics from a limited religious perspective, but because he used Christian morals as his personal code of conduct in bureaucratic and humanitarian affairs.

5

Vietnam

In the United States today, many students are merely taught the basics of the Vietnam War, with a primary emphasis on the evils of communism. Over the decades that followed the conflict, American textbooks ranged from a small percentage that glorified the war to more than a third that referred to it as "hellish." In the 1970s, most instructional material about the war did not focus on the experience of the individual soldier, but rather referred only to the United States' armed forces, thus removing the human experience from the conversation.[268]

A 1995 *Los Angeles Times* article reported the experience of educators: "Once too controversial to be taught in American high schools, the Vietnam War has slowly slipped into the curriculum, but only in a superficial way. Although many teachers consider Vietnam crucial to understanding American foreign policy and identify it as one of the key events in U.S. history, today's high school students learn about the Vietnam War in much the same way they study other contemporary affairs—quickly and without much depth."[269]

After the Geneva Agreements of 1954, the United States had taken financial and military responsibility for South Vietnam post-French colonial rule. It wasn't until the Front National de Libération du Sud-Viêt Nam (the National Liberation Front, also known as Viet Cong) incited guerilla warfare in the south in 1963, and North Vietnamese and American ships clashed in the controversial Gulf of Tonkin incident, that the United States escalated the stationing of troops in South Vietnam in 1964. The communist regimes of the USSR and the People's Republic of China came to the aid of Ho Chi Minh while anti-communist allies came to the side of South Vietnam. The outbreak of the war thus came to the forefront of the global anti-communist versus communist conflict.

One of the many aspects of the war that is rarely discussed in American schools, however, is how some individuals tried desperately to end the war before its escalation. A few books reveal those early efforts for peace: *Marigold: The Lost Chance for Peace in Vietnam* by James Hershberg, *The Secret Search for Peace in Vietnam* by David Kraslow and Stuart H. Loory, and *Con La Pira in Viet Nam* by Mario Primicerio. Primicerio's book is a firsthand account of La Pira's meeting with President Ho Chi Minh and Prime Minister Pham Van Dong on November 11, 1965. Primicerio, at 25 years old, accompanied La Pira on that momentous occasion as his personal secretary.

According to *The Secret Search for Peace in Vietnam*, La Pira's trip to the Southeast Asian country was conceived of in May 1965 after his friend Fanfani (then Minister of Foreign Affairs) had a meeting with US President Lyndon B. Johnson, in which Johnson is said to have asked Fanfani to assist the United States in "seeking a negotiated settlement."[270] La Pira had already been working on a final document for disarmament and peace since he had been a keynote speaker at a symposium in Moscow in December 1963.[271]

In April 1965, the symposium reconvened, this time taking place in the sixteenth-century fortress of Forte di Belvedere in Florence; the gathering was christened Organization for World Political Studies. Those in attendance, noted the *Spokane Spokesman-Review*, included British Labor Party members Lord Fenner Brockway and William Warbey and French socialist and former Deputy Prime Minister Jules Moch. La Pira presented his ideas about peace talks earnestly and was quoted later on stating that, during the symposium, "an objective political analysis was made of all the documents concerning the crisis . . . and were received with interest in responsible quarters."[272]

A peace appeal, signed by La Pira and Lord Brockway in 1965, was sent to the governments of the states directly involved in the conflict as well as those involved in the Geneva Conference of 1954. The document was said to be broadly ignored except by the North Vietnamese. The Geneva Conference, in an attempt to settle issues of the Korean War and First Indochina War, had resulted in the removal of French Union forces from Hanoi and had generated a split between Ho Chi Minh's Communist North Vietnam and French-colonialist-ruled South Vietnam. North Vietnam signed the Geneva Agreement, even though Ho Chi Minh did not want to institute another election and surrender his victory, while the United States and South Vietnam refused to sign. The core reason for their rejection was fear of over-whelming support for Ho Chi Minh in an election and a subsequent communist takeover. The *Spokesman-Review* reported that the appeal sent by La Pira hoped to address these outstanding issues, and it was answered by Ho Chi Minh, who, in a letter to La Pira, "[expressed] thanks for the interest taken in the problems of his people."[273]

According to La Pira, the intense interest and support that followed the symposium resulted in his seeking an invitation from Ho Chi Minh, undaunted that other diplomats' attempts to visit with the Vietnamese leader had been rejected. After several months of arduous preparation, Ho Chi Minh accepted La Pira's proposal. With that, on October 20, 1965, La Pira headed off to Hanoi with Primicerio at his side. Primicerio said that the journey certainly contained a handful of "adventurous" moments.[274] Their propeller-driven twin-engine aircraft made stops in Warsaw, Moscow, and Beijing; while flying over Mongolia they were hit by a severe storm, which caused them to delay in Irkutsk, Siberia. According to an interview La Pira granted to the leftist publication *LeSpresso*, he had "no comment" regarding his trip to Hanoi, maintaining that it was "strictly a private trip."[275]

Italians . . . Said to Have Been Intermediaries in Overture[276]

Richard Dudman, a Washington and foreign correspondent, spent thirty-one years with the *St. Louis Post-Dispatch*, covering major events such as Fidel Castro's revolution in Cuba, the assassination of John F. Kennedy in Dallas, and, for twelve years, the Vietnam War. In 1970, Dudman was captured along with two other journalists while reporting in Cambodia. Dudman supposedly told the other captives: "If we get out of this alive, we'll have one hell of a good story." Fortunately, all three journalists were released after six weeks, and Dudman detailed his harrowing account in his book *40 Days with the Enemy*.[277]

On Friday, December 17, 1965, Dudman wrote a story in the *Post-Dispatch* about a meeting that took place in Vietnam between former mayor of Florence Giorgio La Pira and the president of North Vietnam, Ho Chi Minh. The story, "Nov.12 Hanoi Peace Move Reported Rejected by U.S.," explained how two Italians, Giorgio La Pira and Mario Primicerio, brought back a new peace proposal to the United States government after their nearly two-hour meeting in Hanoi. The essence of the conversation with President Ho Chi Minh, as recounted by the Italians, revolved around their push for a "unilateral cease-fire, including cessation of all bombing." Ho Chi Minh responded that, he "[would] be at the negotiating table the next day," which La Pira and Primicerio saw as a step toward diplomatic communication and away from further military involvement.[278]

False reports circulated about how La Pira and Ho Chi Minh communicated, pinning the young Primicerio as a linguist who acted as their translator, speaking French with Ho Chi Minh and then translating his dialogue into Italian for La Pira. The truth was that La Pira and Ho were both fluent in French and conversed without the need for an interpreter.

After describing the meeting and Ho Chi Minh's willingness to negotiate a peace deal, Dudman's article disclosed the contradictory responses from the US government. It was affirmed at first that the United States had rejected the report in early December, but then a formal response from the State Department proclaimed otherwise, confirming the talks had been taken very seriously. Yet, the *St. Louis Post-Dispatch* was later contacted by a White House official who confirmed that the peace proposal was "looked at carefully" but was "not taken very seriously," adding that the department gave little credibility to the peace-keeping efforts of La Pira and an American emissary, whom La Pira had called upon to confirm the talks on his behalf.[279]

This emissary, an American lawyer, had given the Johnson administration a message detailing La Pira's conversation with President Ho a week prior to the publication of Dudman's article. The lawyer claimed that he had spent four hours discussing the matter with La Pira and Primicerio in Italy. The main points had been compiled into a memo and distributed throughout the branches of the US government, landing on the desks of leaders in the White House, foreign policy executives in the State Department, and certain members of Congress. A note at the end of the memo stressed the importance of keeping the matter confidential: "The Italians [felt] that, while Ho Chi Minh wanted his views made known to American leaders, he would, because of Chinese pressure, have to deny them if they were attributed to him publicly."[280]

At the time of Dudman's reporting, publicity was thought to be the only way the Johnson administration would be deterred from fulfilling its pledge to seek a military solution in Vietnam. Exposing government actions to the public would put the necessary pressure on the administration to seek new resolutions, in particular considering Hanoi's continued gestures expressing their desire to negotiate. If the press exposed Johnson's administration for rejecting Ho's outreach, there would be upheaval from the American public about prolonging the war. All the same, Dudman wrote that there were those within the Johnson administration who believed that Beijing was demanding that Hanoi achieve military success in South Vietnam. Rumor had it that the North Vietnamese held a public position and a private position, the former motivating Ho to likely deny his conversation with La Pira and Primicerio. The lawyer confirmed the theory, insisting that Hanoi welcomed negotiations but was under pressure from China and afraid of appearing weak.[281]

The lawyer's memorandum relayed his conversation with La Pira, who recalled Ho Chi Minh saying that the "withdrawal of American troops was not a precondition of negotiations." Ho's eagerness to be at the negotiating table "the next day" did depend on two requirements being met, which were only feasible after the United States halted the fighting and bombing. First, the United States would have to negotiate with the armed communist political organization in South Vietnam, the National Liberation Front (NLF), and second, the United States would have to be inclined to discuss the four points of compromise which were said to be the main topic of discussion during La Pira and Ho's meeting.[282]

According to North Vietnamese Prime Minister Pham Van Dong, his government was strictly adhering to the 1954 Geneva Agreement, but to move forward on a peaceful settlement, the United States would have to adhere to the four-point program that was presented to them as well. The points were summarized by Dudman as follows:

1. United States military withdrawal from South Vietnam and a cessation of all attacks in North and South Vietnam.

2. Neutralization of North and South Vietnam pending reunification.

3. Settlement of the internal affairs of South Vietnam "by the South Vietnamese people themselves, in accordance with the program of the NLF."

4. Peaceful reunification by the Vietnamese people in both zones without any foreign interference.[283]

It was La Pira's understanding, Dudman writes, that "the war could [end] before a substantial increase in Chinese influence in Vietnam occurred." La Pira hypothesized that "Vietnam [could] be the most independent communist country in the world, with the possible exception of Yugoslavia, and that it could be one of the best friends to the west."[284]

A warning was issued from the North Vietnamese that any bombing of Haiphong or Hanoi would eliminate the possibility of a negotiated settlement, as reported by the unnamed American lawyer. La Pira emphasized that "the Italian government and the Vatican knew of his trip and were highly pleased by its results," generating further support of evidence that peace talks had occurred.[285]

On December 10, 1965, an official Vietnamese news agency released a statement, which Dudman included in his piece, that differed greatly from the civil response of Ho Chi Minh and Pham van Dong as relayed by the American lawyer. The statement claimed the talks were simply "a trick to appease public opinion . . . a maneuver to prepare further expansion of the war." It was a perfect example of the contradictory accounts of Hanoi's public and private stance.[286]

Dudman's sprawling piece finished with how US Secretary of State Dean Rusk responded to the peace feeler report during a press conference on December 9, 1965, where he expressed that he welcomed negotiations from the Vietnamese, stating: "Come to the table. . . . Reconvene the Geneva conference of 1954. Let each party . . . say what he has on [his] mind . . . then take a look at the

situation . . . and see whether there is any basis for peace."
When pressured to either confirm or deny if a cease-fire
was in order, Rusk responded that it was difficult to answer
that type of question during a short press conference given
the complexities of the situation. He did say that "a cease-
fire could be [the] first order of business," but believed that
to truly begin the peace process, they would have to "pull
North Vietnam and South Vietnam apart militarily."[287]

On the same front page as Dudman's article, the
Associated Press ran with the bold headline "Rusk Asks for
Clarification of Hanoi 'Feeler' from Fanfani." The article
stated that even before the American lawyer approached
the administration in Washington, Amintore Fanfani—
the only Italian to have held the position of President
of the United Nations General Assembly—delivered a
letter to President Johnson on November 20, 1965. In
the correspondence, he confirmed La Pira's statement
that "the government of Hanoi was prepared to initiate
negotiations without first requiring actual withdrawal of
the American troops."[288]

Dudman's story covering La Pira's meeting spread
like wildfire throughout the US press, and for the following weeks created tension between the governments of the
United States and Italy, the latter apprehensive toward the
former over how Italian mediation efforts transpired. The
event even challenged the personal life of one Italian government official, with dramatics playing out in almost soap
opera fashion.

The *New York Times* picked up on Dudman's story
and ran a condensed version of events the next day with

the header: "Italian Ex-Mayor Active Diplomat." La Pira's role as a "peace feeler" was reported as commonplace for the most "colorful and controversial political figures" in Italian politics. Reporter Arnold H. Lubash wrote that La Pira often tried to operate as a mediator in international conflicts and spoke with "deep conviction and rushing enthusiasm of the need for peace and brotherhood."[289]

Lubash rehashed the meeting of November 11, consolidating Fanfani's correspondence with President Johnson into one small paragraph. A majority of the article covered the fact that La Pira's "unconventional tactics and tolerance of Communists [had] aroused criticism," including how La Pira described his own views on communism as "realistic, rather than visionary." Lubash quoted La Pira as saying: "There is only one way to eradicate Communism from Italy and the world, that is to prove ourselves earnest defenders of the humble classes to the very end."[290]

A literal translation of the essential elements

On the same day Lubash's story ran, the *Spokane Spokesman-Review* revealed that Fanfani had received a letter from Mario Primicerio in New York on November 19, 1965, which had been written by La Pira, and had translated the sentiment succinctly into English. The letter explained the details of the talk with Ho Chi Minh on November 11. In urgency, Fanfani met with US Ambassador Arthur J. Goldberg the following morning, "in view of the importance of the problem." Fanfani expressed that it was his obligation and considered it extremely necessary to provide Goldberg a letter of "a literal translation of the essential elements" regarding La Pira's communications with the communist leader, stressing that it should be handed directly to President Johnson.[291] Based on a chronological ordering of letters and meeting dates, Fanfani was therefore the first of La Pira's contacts to pressure the Johnson administration into action.

Fanfani's letter to President Johnson, per a "Draft Memorandum From Secretary of State Rusk to President Johnson" from November 24, 1965, was a paraphrased account of events. Rusk claimed that the Fanfani letter addressed to President Johnson was "a careful official translation . . . which was addressed to . . . [President Johnson] through Ambassador Goldberg, on which Goldberg informed Valenti"[292] (Jack Valenti was Special Assistant to President Johnson). The letter, which was not published in the original *Spokesman-Review* article, reads as follows:

New York, November 20, 1965
The President of the General Assembly

Mr. President:

In the interview which you graciously accorded me at the end of May you repeated anew your firm intention to seek assiduously a negotiated solution for the conflict in Vietnam.

In the hope of being able to assist in the realization of this noble purpose, I bring to your attention the following.

On Thursday, November 11, in Hanoi, Ho Chi Minh and the President of the Council, Van Dong, expressed to two persons (known to me) the strong desire to find a peaceful solution to the conflict in Vietnam and, in summary, stated—according to what they wrote me—that "in order for the peace negotiations to come about, there will be necessary (a) a cease-fire (by air, by sea, by land) in the entire territory of Vietnam (north and south); the cessation, that is, of all belligerent operations (including therefore also the cessation of debarkation of further American troops); (b) a declaration according to which the Geneva Agreements of 1954 will be taken as the basis for the negotiations—a declaration made up of the four points formulated by Hanoi, points that are in reality the explanation of the Geneva text and which, therefore, can be reduced to a single point: application in other words, of the Geneva Accords."

The text of the communication which I have received adds that "the Government in Hanoi is prepared to initiate negotiations without first requiring actual withdrawal of the American troops."

To the same interlocutors Ho Chi Minh said: "I am prepared to go anywhere; to meet anyone."

These are the essential points that one of the two interlocutors of Ho Chi Minh and Van Dong sent me in writing last night and which, in this letter of mine—confided to Mr. A. Goldberg, the US representative to the UN, so that he can deliver it promptly and confidentially—I bring word for word to your attention.

You surely have other elements by which to judge the importance of the above. As President of the 20th Assembly, as a high official of Italy, as a sincere friend of the United States and of yourself, I hope that this contribution to the sought-for peaceful solution, always more necessary and more urgent, may be a useful one. And I am at your disposition for any step that you consider opportune in the matter.

With sincere pleasure at your recovery and with best wishes for your high mission, I send my respectful greetings.

Yours,

(Signed) Amintore Fanfani[293]

According to the *Spokesman-Review*, Fanfani said that Goldberg presented him with a response from Secretary Rusk, from which he translated urgently that very night the "essential elements" and sent them in a personal letter to President Ho Chi Minh. A week later, on December 13, Fanfani notified Rusk that he had delivered the translated letter to a certified representative of Hanoi on December 8, but that "no answer . . . [had] reached him as of today."[294]

The article states that Fanfani, per the original request of the United States, had upheld the "strictest secrecy on [the] matter . . . in order not to jeopardize any possible constructive outcome." Fanfani remained tight-lipped about whether the publication of the talks "jeopardized chances for peace," even after the US government eventually leaked the information and confirmed Fanfani as an intermediary.[295]

It is never mentioned who originally leaked the information about the secretive peace talks to Dudman, as published in his piece on December 17. This remained an important unanswered question, considering that the higher-ups in both the United States and Vietnam had expressed wishes to keep peace talks under wraps and out of the public eye.

Hanoi calls Peace Bid U.S. Hoax

Douglas Kiker's piece "Hanoi calls Peace Bid U.S. Hoax" was published on December 19, 1965, in the *Boston Globe*. The article disclosed that during a Radio Hanoi broadcast, the North Vietnamese accused the Johnson administration of "sheer groundless fabrications" over the report of possible peace negotiations, insisting that the administration publicized the report in an effort to "camouflage new military steps." There was no immediate response from the White House, only that they were "toying" with the idea of submitting a reply. Kiker reported that the White House had just the day before agonized over the premature leak of the communiqué, describing La Pira's report as the most "promising" signal for peace in a long time.[296]

The story continued on page five with the headline: "Italian Reasserts Ho's Words." Kiker reported that on December 18, additional concurrent developments had unfolded. In Florence, the Italians, who had delivered what they considered an accurate peace feeler from North Vietnam, accused the United States of sabotaging the entire proposition.[297]

So, who leaked the information about the talks? Fingers were pointed firmly at Secretary of State Dean Rusk. Primicerio was quoted as saying, "Rusk . . . wanted the mission to fail by disclosing in advance what had been done."[298] But Primicerio strongly denied this account, saying that he "never expressed any judgment to any journalist regarding State Secretary Rusk."[299] The *New York Times*, on December 20, wrote that the correspondent who had the conversation with Primicerio affirmed that the statement was quoted accurately.[300] As for the Radio Hanoi broadcast that had dismissed the negotiations, La Pira said: "I confirm that I and Prof. Mario Primicerio, when we were received on Nov. 11 in Hanoi, heard from President Ho Chi Minh's own voice that he was prepared for the good of his people to go anywhere and meet anyone to negotiate for peace."[301]

In an effort to keep the peace talks alive between the North Vietnamese and US governments, Amintore Fanfani set up a meeting with Dean Rusk. However, it was reported by White House administration officials that the meeting with Fanfani had already been scheduled, "primarily in his capacity as foreign minister," with the expectation by Fanfani that the Vietnam dilemma was to be discussed.[302] Still, there was supposition around the administration salvaging preliminary negotiations.

Kiker then references the *St. Louis Post-Dispatch*, which had first reported on the peace probe. The *Post-Dispatch* claimed that the bombing of an electrical plant in Haiphong on December 15 was the result of Hanoi not responding to Secretary Rusk's letter, which had been sent by Fanfani and was only received on December 13. President Johnson, as reported in the *Post-Dispatch*, had been notified well ahead of the bombing, and was aware that such a strike could "close the door on negotiations." Ambassador Goldberg defended the actions of the bombing, stressing that the accusation of carrying out a strike while negotiations were open was "totally irresponsible, absolutely untrue, and an invention from first to last." The Johnson administration also appeared to distance themselves from the negotiation attempts represented by Rusk's letter, adding: "We are not such fools that we would not give them more than two days to prepare a reply."[303]

New York Attorney Told of Ho's Peace Move

Two days after Dudman's article, the emissary who delivered the memorandum to the Johnson administration was revealed to be New York lawyer Peter Weiss, President of the American Committee on Africa. Formed in 1953, the committee provided active support for the emancipation of Africa by promoting self-government and educational assistance, and in 1965 actively opposed the policies of apartheid in South Africa.

The *New York Times*, on December 19, 1965, published a feature by M.S. Handler entitled "New York Lawyer Tells of Role As Transmitter of Hanoi 'Feeler,'"[304] and it described, in great detail, the role Weiss played in the peace overture. Handler had been the bureau chief for the United Press in Bonn, Germany, but returned home after World War II to cover the civil rights movement. He built close relationships with Rev. Dr. Martin Luther King Jr., as well as other Black leaders, which led to him writing the introduction for the autobiography of Malcolm X.[305] Throughout the *Times* interview, Handler was able to shed light on how Weiss found himself in the middle of an international conflict.

Handler explained that Weiss had met La Pira in 1961 during a meeting of the Mediterranean Colloquium, an organization focused on reducing tensions between Israel and Arab nations. Weiss arrived in France on December 3, 1965, and had plans to return to New York after his business trip in Strasbourg when he received an urgent phone call from La Pira asking him to come to Florence.[306]

Weiss told La Pira that he was going back to New York, to which La Pira replied: "It is a critical moment in history and you are called upon to play a role, you must find a way to come here." Weiss was convinced of the urgency of the matter and took the next train from Strasbourg to Florence, arriving at noon the following day. He met La Pira in a clinic, assumed to be the one owned by his friend Professor Palumbo, with whom La Pira would stay during the winter. The pair talked for nearly four hours and were joined halfway through by Mario Primicerio.[307]

La Pira explained to Weiss the details of the November 11 meeting with North Vietnamese leaders and two colonels representing the NLF. According to Handler, Weiss characterized La Pira as a man possessed with a "volatile personality with strong moral compulsions," which varied greatly from his description of Primicerio's "cold reasoning mind." La Pira told Weiss that throughout the meeting "he had a feeling that Ho Chi Minh was trying to convey his willingness to end the war on terms acceptable to Hanoi." According to the Italians, Weiss continued, Ho alluded to the tremendous suffering of his country due to frequent bombings by the Americans and said, "The 17th parallel goes straight through my heart."[308]

Weiss recounted La Pira's feeling that Ho was waiting for action from the US government but was not willing to "haggle" over the specifics or initiate the peace process. Weiss explained to La Pira that he would be unable to meet with President Johnson, to which La Pira responded: "You must see Goldberg, he is a good man, I have faith in Goldberg. You must see others who are in a position to influence President Johnson." La Pira implored him: "You must see Bundy, Fulbright and Senators, you know best. It's up to you. Use this information as you see fit." Even though Fanfani had been pushing La Pira's message to his contacts in Washington, La Pira stressed to Weiss that time was of the essence and a solution was far too "critical to wait."[309]

Upon arriving back in New York on December 6, Weiss set up a meeting with Arthur J. Goldberg for December 8 to personally hand him the written account of his conversation with La Pira. Weiss said he told Goldberg that the contents of the account would "not be news to him."[310] After reaching Goldberg, Weiss made copies of the summary and passed them out to other influential high-ranking government officials.

Weiss stated, "In [my] view, the Hanoi 'message' was not truly a 'peace feeler,' but a restatement of a well-known position." He concluded the interview by affirming that when the current matter diminished, Hanoi would be open to peace talks.[311]

The *Boston Globe* reported that Weiss "denied emphatically that he had 'leaked' the story to the *St. Louis Post-Dispatch*," adding that a *Post-Dispatch* reporter had reached out to him on December 8, to ask about his involvement. Weiss affirmed that he pleaded with the reporter to "not run the story."[312]

LAWYER MEETS EMISSARY:
YANK TELLS ROLE IN PEACE BID[313]
December 19, 1965 - *Courier-Journal*, Louisville, KY

LAWYER DELIVERS ITALIAN'S MESSAGE[314]
December 19, 1965 - *Daily Oklahoman*, Oklahoma, OK

NEW YORK ATTORNEY TOLD
OF HO'S PEACE MOVE[315]
December 19, 1965 - *Chicago Tribune*, Chicago, IL

La Pira Is Old Hand At Politics

Leo J. Wollemborg—an Italian, naturalized American citizen, journalist, and Holocaust survivor—returned to Rome after the war, where he was a correspondent for more than thirty years for various newspapers, including the *Washington Post*. In his December 1965 piece, "La Pira Is Old Hand At Politics," published in the *Boston Globe*, Wollemborg writes that La Pira's opponents had nicknamed him "the disarmed prophet" and a "20th century Savonarola." Harsher critics, according to Wollemborg, called La Pira a "tool or a willing stooge of the Communist both in Italy . . . and on the international stage."[316]

The former mayor was quoted professing that "the law must give way before the gospel." Wollemborg describes La Pira as a devout Catholic, committed to building bridges "between the communist and western world" and skilled at organizing support "both popular and political" for causes he defended.[317]

The article disclosed that La Pira was backed by influential members within the Catholic Church and its diplomatic branches. The news circulating the week of December

13, 1965, was that the Vatican had been attempting to end the fighting in Vietnam or, at the very least, procure a truce over the upcoming Christmas holiday.[318]

Wollemborg determined that La Pira's true intention was to have the communist People's Republic of China take part in arms control talks, which could lead to their admission to the United Nations. It was also Wollemborg's understanding that La Pira was attempting to establish Florence as the global political nerve center, considering that, in La Pira's words, "the establishment and projected activities of the world political center [were] responsible for his being invited the [previous] month to Hanoi."[319] Under the pretense of world peace, as Wollemborg saw it, La Pira had cultivated a diplomatic reputation for Florence that was bolstered by the American press's frequent coverage of the city's hometown hero.

Wollemborg noted that "a young and brilliant instructor in nuclear physics and mathematics at the University of Florence" by the name of Mario Primicerio had accompanied La Pira on the trip to Vietnam as his close confidant. He added that it was the young Primicerio who had traveled to New York to hand deliver a letter (the one which detailed their talks with the Vietnamese leaders) to another dear friend of La Pira, Amintore Fanfani.[320]

La Pira and Ho Chi Minh had previously met in France a few years earlier, Wollemborg revealed. La Pira and others close to him believed Ho Chi Minh and Pham Van Dong to be "national communists with a background in Western European culture," both determined to find a "political solution" in Vietnam. Wollemborg suggested that this long-standing relationship could be why Ho was so quick to accept La Pira's diplomatic aid in 1965.[321]

International reporter and United Nations correspondent for the *St. Louis Post-Dispatch* Donald Grant drew parallels between La Pira and Primicerio's peace talk and another that took place a month earlier between Hungarian foreign minister Janos Peter and Ho Chi Minh. Peter's peace appeal was also rejected by Secretary of State Dean Rusk.[322]

It was divulged to the *St. Louis Post-Dispatch* that Peter had been thoroughly briefed by North Vietnamese representatives from Hanoi, as well as the National Liberation Front, regarding their will to enter negotiations, but that Ambassador Goldberg, during a peace conference, insisted that "no message from Hanoi" had been delivered by any intermediaries. The US government had rejected a peace offer even earlier, in 1964, after UN Secretary General U Thant proposed a meeting with Ho Chi Minh in Rangoon, Burma. The notice bearing the United States' rejection of the peace appeal arrived in Hanoi just as the United States began an onslaught of bombing in North Vietnam.[323] Nevertheless, the meeting between the two Italians and the North Vietnamese continued to dominate headlines in newspapers across America, even as information about the appeals sent by other intermediaries began to surface.

WILL PREMATURE DISCLOSURE OF OFFER HALT PEACE TALKS[324]
December 18, 1965 - *Spokesman-Review*, Spokane, WA

HANOI PEACE FEELER IS BRANDED A HOAX:
EMISSARY VOWS U.S. KILLED TRY[325]
December 19, 1965 - *Vernon Daily Record,* Vernon, TX

DID U.S. COOL PEACE MOVE?[326]
December 19, 1965 - *Tennessean,* Nashville, TN

HANOI ACCUSES U.S OF HOAX:
ITALIAN INSISTS HO DID OFFER PEACE TALKS
AS HE REPORTED[327]
December 19, 1965 - *Independent Press-Telegram,*
Long Beach, CA

BUT MINH SAYS
'PEACE:' REDS SAY U.S. IN PEACE HOAX[328]
December 19, 1965 - *Alamogordo Daily News,*
Alamogordo, NM

HANOI DENIES LEADERS
MADE PEACE OFFERS[329]
December 19, 1965 - *Casper Star-Tribune,* Casper, WY

Storm Over U.S. Report On Peace Bid[330]

Dean Rusk had once described Pulitzer-Prize-winning Associated Press correspondent John M. Hightower as "the most capable and best informed reporter [he had] ever seen."[331] The *Oakland Tribune* published Hightower's reports of the controversy the Johnson administration found itself in after Richard Dudman and the *St. Louis Post-Dispatch* exposed the US government's rejection of a viable new peace bid from North Vietnam.[332]

Hightower elaborated on the State Department's reaction to Primicerio's allegedly blaming Rusk for divulging the mission to the press. Rusk deemed the allegations "outrageous" and was described as being "angered and upset by the criticism." Hightower writes that Goldberg seemed unconcerned that the leak of the talks could possibly kill the ongoing peace negotiations and quoted the UN ambassador as saying, "If there is a genuine desire on both sides to negotiate, that desire will surmount whatever the difficulties are of disclosure."[333]

La Pira continued to affirm that the offer had been made by Ho Chi Minh, even as Hanoi adamantly denied that any "peace feeler" had been sent in the first place. Critics were starting to speak out against the Johnson administration, which had been caught "avoiding negotiations." Dr. Benjamin Spock and H. Stuart Hughes, members of the Committee for a Sane Nuclear Policy, believed the administration was trying to "keep the National Liberation Front . . . out of any future government in Saigon."[334]

The United States' decision to publish the letters of the "peace-seeking mission" confused La Pira, who reiterated to the Catholic paper *L'avvenire d'Italia*: "I think that official secrecy would have been more useful." The *Spokane Spokesman-Review*, on December 21, 1965, drew from a report out of Rome via Reuters, quoting La Pira's response to the refutations by Hanoi: "It [was] necessary to read the documents attentively. Distinctions must be made between the two documents in Hanoi." La Pira summarized the contradictory statements made by Hanoi, saying, "The first, of strictly diplomatic nature, denied that there had been peace soundings on the part of the Hanoi government. The second, on the other hand, contains the essential ideas of my talks with the North Vietnam leaders without contradicting what I have affirmed."[335]

Critics did not only speak out against the Johnson administration. Back home in Italy, Foreign Minister Fanfani was criticized for promoting "false peace hopes," and his acceptance of the peace talks in Hanoi was described as "ridiculous, not to say grotesque." The *Casper Star-Tribune* from Wyoming, on December 22, 1965, published a report provided by United Press International (UPI) which revealed that opponents of Fanfani were accusing him of a "lack of judgment."[336] Fanfani's critics believed that he should not have passed along La Pira's impression of the talks to government officials in Washington. By 1965, however, Fanfani and La Pira had been close friends for more than twenty years; one could surmise that Fanfani completely believed the message La Pira had delivered after his visit to Hanoi, particularly considering its magnitude.

A few days passed in late December before the story was picked up again, this time out of Italy, from which Pope Paul VI sent a plea for peace to the three nations involved in the conflict.

The day after Christmas 1965, *New York Times* Rome Bureau Chief Robert C. Doty reported on Pope Paul VI's pure joy over the thirty-hour Christmas truce between

North and South Vietnam and the United States. In a speech to thousands in St. Peter's Square, the pontiff spoke of how high hopes had been renewed over the "agreement to preserve peace in Vietnam on Christmas."[337]

Doty wrote that La Pira's trip to Hanoi in November could have played a part in the Viet Cong agreeing to a Christmas truce on December 7. Unable to reach La Pira for comment, Doty spoke with Primicerio, who said that during their meeting with Ho Chi Minh, "they discussed every possible opening toward peace . . . negotiations, truce, etc."[338] It was also during this Christmas holiday that Fanfani set a date to explain to his parliamentary critics how he became involved as the middleman.

The peace feeler controversy was heating up within the Italian government, as they sat stuck between denials in Hanoi and hesitation in Washington. The *Baltimore Sun*, on December 27, 1965, headlined that Fanfani was to explain the disputed "peace feeler" and that a "special session was called to hear [his] role as middleman." The session was scheduled for January 7, 1966, wherein the Chamber of Deputies Foreign Affairs Commission would deliberate the charges of whether Fanfani was "gullible" or "acted with the knowledge of the Italian Government."[339]

Fanfani, a "political warrior," was known not to back down when confronted, and was wholeheartedly convinced that passing on La Pira's message from Hanoi was the correct thing to do. La Pira was asked if he thought the United States had been ingenious in their exposing of his talk in Hanoi; he replied that "it probably put Ho under hard pressure from [Beijing]."[340]

Pressure was also mounting for Fanfani, as reported by the *Baltimore Sun*, which claimed that tremendous stress had been placed on Italian Prime Minister Aldo Moro and the fragile balance in the center-left government of Christian Democrats and Socialists. The Italian Republican Party questioned if the government believed "operetta type initiatives" were "in conformity with the gravity of the situation." Other political parties demanded that Moro's government intercede with the American government, "so that it [would] accept the proposals of Ho Chi Minh entrusted to Prof. La Pira and [which] Fanfani transmitted to the United States."[341]

The *Baltimore Sun* quoted the Italian Socialist Party newspaper the *Avanti* as saying: "La Pira may have put a bit of candor and naivety into the gesture, but when candor and naivety are put at the service of peace, everything becomes worthy and even moving." [342]

Wife's Meddling

The controversy eventually infiltrated Fanfani's own home and personal relationships. His wife, Bianca Rosa, was said to have complicated things after she "meddled" in the Vietnam affair.[343] The so-called "meddling" was due to an incident that took place during a private dinner party she organized at their home. In an effort to set the record straight on the peace invitation, and possibly ease the tension surrounding her husband, Bianca invited La Pira and Gianna Preda, editor of the right-wing newspaper

Il Borghese, to her home. It was reported in the *New York Daily News* that Bianca, who had a "deep admiration for La Pira . . . believed he would be able to convert the right-wing editor to his leftist beliefs."[344]

Unfortunately for Bianca, the plan backfired and caused more harm than good. *Il Borghese*, under the headline "Keep Bianca Rosa from ever mixing in Politics," quoted La Pira as bad-mouthing Secretary of State Dean Rusk, saying Rusk "does not understand anything." La Pira was quoted by Preda as calling Moro "soft" and Fanfani an "Italian de Gaulle."[345] The *Tucson Daily Citizen* ran the story of the dinner party gone awry, adding that Fanfani expressed sharp criticism over Bianca's actions, calling the party an "imprudent initiative."[346]

La Pira sincerely denied that he had given any such interview, and rather explained that he merely "met a lady unknown" to him at the Fanfani residence, as reported by the *Casper [WY] Star-Tribune*.[347] The remarks were "tongue-in-cheek observations,"[348] according to La Pira. Preda, after hearing of La Pira's denial, called him "the holy liar"[349] and said she felt free to publish his remarks because he "had not converted her."[350]

The political turmoil and the reports of Bianca's imped-ing diplomatic matters resulted in Fanfani's submitting his resignation over what he called "unjust accusations." The *Fresno [CA] Bee*, on December 28, 1965, published the story under the headline: "Fanfani Quits Italy Job, Blames Viet Issue, Wife's Meddling." Fanfani was quoted calling his resignation "irrevocable," even after Prime Minister Moro refused to accept it.[351]

The *Sheboygan [WI] Press* published an article on December 29, 1965, by foreign correspondent Rufus S. Goodwin, also claiming to know the reason Fanfani announced his resignation. Goodwin reported that, in Fanfani's resignation letter, he blamed his wife of twenty-six years, Bianca Rosa, and his dear friend Giorgio La Pira for his resignation, and was desperately trying to dissociate himself from La Pira's criticism of Secretary Rusk.[352]

Reluctantly, Moro finally accepted Fanfani's resignation, leading some to believe the coalition between the Christian Democrats and Socialists would now fail.[353] The next day, Italian President Giuseppe Saragat added an additional title to Moro's resume for the time being: Foreign Minister.

The announcement of Fanfani's resignation and the ongoing turmoil within the Italian government made its way to the White House. During a phone conversation between Under Secretary of State George Ball and President Johnson on December 28, 1965, Ball mentioned that "Goldberg [was leaving for Rome that night]," but that "Fanfani tendered his resignation today to Moro over the La Pira incident, and apparently it appears that the Italian Government is in a shaky position." Ball continued that he "was concerned that since Goldberg was associated with Fanfani in the La Pira incident that the Italian press would say we are interfering in domestic politics."[354]

Everybody's Mad at Everybody

Mary McGrory's opinion of Bianca Rosa Fanfani's attempt to help the critics on the right better understand her husband's motives was that of an "unauthorized Dove." Under the headline "Everybody's Mad at Everybody," McGrory wrote in the *Boston Globe* that those close to Bianca were baffled by her behavior. But she then qualified Bianca's actions by adding that "devoted wives are often convinced they can do the job better . . . [seeing] the timid husband when he should be bold." Bianca, according to McGrory, took a "roundabout" approach to get the meeting between La Pira and "the lady editor of the blackly right-wing journal." To put things in terms of American diplomacy, McGrory said the meeting was equivalent to Lady Bird Johnson arranging a dinner party in order for conservative William F. Buckley and her husband's political advisor, Democratic Party organizer Bobby Baker, to meet.[355]

La Pira was told by Bianca that he would be meeting a woman with spiritual doubts, and he, being a spectacularly religious man, as McGrory wrote, jumped at the opportunity, behaving like Fulton Sheen, the American bishop known for his work on radio and television. The talk was reported to have gone smoothly on a "worldly level" but, McGrory observed, "for the visionary he is supposed to be, La Pira has observed his fellow man with much trenchancy."[356]

The feud within the Fanfani household caused McGrory to ponder if the couple were still speaking to each other, considering that it was obvious who was at fault.

McGrory finished by stating that even as Amintore Fanfani peers out over the Vatican, the "most clamorous Italian Dove of all, Pope Paul VI, is still on the wing, high above the battle with life tenure besides."[357]

Over the course of the next couple of days, the commission that was to hear Fanfani explain his involvement in the peace talks overture was canceled due to his resignation. The Italian Communist Party urged Moro to step down as well. Communist leaders were attempting to secure a "no confidence motion" in parliament over the "red hot" foreign policy issues that "should have led to a government crisis," pointing in particular to La Pira's "embarrassing remarks" as published in *Il Borghese*.[358] With a majority of 240 needed, the vote of confidence passed at 325–154, resulting in a victory for Moro and the retention of his position.[359]

One final barrage of criticism over the Vietnam peace feeler was provided by Russell Kirk, whom some had named the "Father of American Conservatism."[360] In his piece "To the Point: On Becoming a Fool in Hanoi" published in the *Bridgeport [CT] Post*, Kirk attacked Fanfani and La Pira vehemently, writing that Fanfani was "always looking for an 'opening to the Left'" and "proceeded to act and talk as though Ho Chi Minh had mellowed and as if the UN could arrange peace in Vietnam." He added that Fanfani "was hideously disillusioned by the prompt mockery of Ho, who denounced La Pira's silliness." Kirk believed that La Pira was "foolish" to think that Ho was keen on ending the war, deducing that such a desire was simply a "figment of [La Pira's] imagination."[361]

Epilogue

After the Storm

On March 2, 1973, the declaration of the International Conference on Vietnam was signed in Paris by US Secretary of State Henry Kissinger and Vietnamese representative Le Duc Tho. Professor Primicerio has revealed that, remarkably, the signed agreement contained the same clauses agreed to in November 1965 by La Pira and Ho Chi Minh.[362]

The story of La Pira's meeting with President Ho Chi Minh arrived on and disappeared from American shores like a hurricane, and like most hurricanes, left damage in its wake. After the meeting, La Pira's political career started to decline, and Bianca Fanfani died in 1968 of an aneurysm at the age of 55. The report of Bianca's death featured in the *El Paso Times* said she had "acutely embarrassed her husband" after arranging the infamous dinner party.[363] However, Amintore Fanfani regained his role as Minister of Foreign Affairs in February 1966 and went on to have a long successful political career, holding several political positions, including President of the Italian Senate and President and Prime Minister (again!) of Italy.

In just twenty-two days, the turmoil surrounding the peace overture was over, and for the most part, so was the coverage of Giorgio La Pira in the US press. Although his name appeared a few more times, it was many years before he would be the focus of the coverage again.

Near the apex of the Vietnam War, on April 1, 1967, the *Sacramento Bee* reported that communist members of the Florence city council were boycotting a reception for Vice President Hubert Humphrey of the United States. At the time, La Pira was the head of a group of Florence intellectuals and, undeterred by past events, he sent a letter to the vice president demanding a halt to the air raids on North Vietnam. This act displayed La Pira's continued determination to stop the killing in South East Asia.[364]

Eight years after La Pira's trip to Hanoi, the *Honolulu Advertiser*, on February 15, 1973, published a story supplied by *Agence France-Presse*. It detailed the meeting between Pope Paul VI and Vietnamese negotiator Xuan Thuy that took place at the Vatican, the first with an official Hanoi representative. After the meeting, the pope spoke in front of three thousand people, reassuring them of Hanoi's peaceful motives. La Pira, who attended a reception at the Vatican honoring Thuy, called the meeting "a great event in history."[365]

One of the last American articles that mentioned La Pira didn't involve the Vietnam event. The *Billings [MT] Gazette* published a story on May 19, 1976, provided by UPI. The story said the Christian Democratic Party was "divided and discredited," emphasizing that they had nominated Fiat Vice President Umberto Agnelli, younger brother of Fiat's principal shareholder Gianni Agnelli, as a senatorial candidate. The Communist Party was growing in popularity with 2.5 million votes in regional elections and was expected to gain its first cabinet seats since the end of the war. In an effort to acquire more of the left-wing Catholic vote, the Christian Democrats persuaded La Pira, the "leftwinger who gave his own overcoats to the poor and bankrupt factories to [their] workers," to come out of political retirement. In spite of growing health problems, La Pira "[agreed] in order to continue the politics of disarmament, unity and peace and to affirm the primacy of human and Christian values in a society growing ever more violent and materialistic."[366] In one last political achievement, he was elected to both the Chamber of Deputies and the Senate for Montevarchi, another Tuscan city; he accepted the position in the Chamber.

Even though he might have been out of the spotlight in the United States, La Pira had continued to travel the world pushing for peaceful resolutions. He was elected president of the World Federation of United Cities (FMCU) in 1967 and traveled to Israel and Egypt for talks with Israeli Foreign Minister Abba Eban, Egyptian President Gamal Abdel Nasser, and the mayors of Hebron and Bethlehem. La Pira was routinely found meeting with the Vietnamese delegation in Helsinki, Moscow, and Stockholm in an effort to speed up the inauguration of the Paris Conference for Peace in Vietnam; he attended the Paris Peace Accords in 1973.[367]

La Pira received coverage for what appears to be the last time in a US newspaper when on November 5, 1977, Giorgio La Pira, "The Saintly Mayor," died of a brain hemorrhage in his beloved city of Florence.[368] The story of his death was carried in multiple newspapers, including the *New York Times,* which ran the AP's report out of Florence. The obituary provided an extremely abridged history of La Pira's multitude of charitable contributions to society over the years, from selling matchboxes to pay for law school, to factory takeovers and helping the poor, to—as reported— his unfortunate "political decline" after the Vietnam episode. The four-paragraph tribute barely scratched the surface of the man La Pira, whom the AP called the "World Peace Crusader."[369] Most obituaries honoring La Pira's death hardly touched on his accomplishments, mainly focusing on his trip to Vietnam and his ascetic lifestyle.

The *Simpson's Leader-Times* out of Kittanning, PA, ran a tribute provided by UPI from Vatican City. The article gets straight to the point of what many were already speculating: "No one [had] said yet, but there is a very good chance that Giorgio La Pira, the former Florence mayor . . . may someday be proclaimed a saint of the Roman Catholic Church."[370] It was reported that Pope Paul VI referred to him as "Dear Prof. Giorgio La Pira, whose profound faith you all know."[371]

Amintore Fanfani, La Pira's dear friend and confidant, was said to have an old hat of La Pira's, and when any of his children became sick, he placed the hat near the child's bed, "as is done with relics of saints."[372]

Acknowledgements

Through perseverance and a lot of luck, I was able to locate some individuals here in the United States connected to Giorgio La Pira. To these people, I want to say thank you for taking the time out of your busy lives to share your stories with me.

I was most astonished to find those who had actually met Giorgio La Pira: Suzy Johnston, whose father was San Mateo Mayor Hugh A. Wayne; and contemporaries of La Pira, including peace activist Cora Weiss. I surprised Sylvia Bockserman with a phone call after I discovered that her husband Julian Bockserman was influenced by La Pira as a young man growing up in Illinois. It was an honor to be able to provide Sylvia and her family with the newspaper clipping featuring Julian's high school graduation speech in which he acknowledged La Pira's accomplishments.

I spoke with and have since developed friendships with Enza Bloise and Frank V. Susino. Enza's father, Santo Matarazzo, was a Brooklyn artist who paid tribute to La

Pira by making a plaster sculpture of him. Matarazzo, a huge admirer of La Pira, felt a kinship to the professor because they were both born in Pozzallo, Sicily. Enza told me in a phone conversation that in August 2005, the bust her father produced of La Pira was put on permanent display in Pozzallo.

Frank Susino, a close friend of the Matarazzo family, is a member of the Society of the Citizens of Pozzallo located in Brooklyn, New York. During my conversation with Frank, he remembered how his mother would share stories of La Pira, and one story in particular: It was said that when La Pira was becoming a more influential, global figure, some former citizens of Pozzallo living in Florence pressed La Pira for assistance, thinking that he would play favorites. The citizens would explain that they hadn't eaten the entire day, to which La Pira, sympathetic to their condition, responded that he knew of people who hadn't eaten in a week.

As mentioned in chapter 1, my family has been involved in every nuance of my discovery of La Pira, a two-year period culminating in this book. My wife Tracy's love, support, and involvement throughout the entire process of putting this book together have been colossal. Without her I don't believe I could have finished it. This opportunity to work with my daughter Molly has been one of the joys of my life. Her creativity in writing and editing has been an inspiration. The many hours we spent together in critical analysis of the material were instrumental in creating a cohesive and comprehensible narrative. She is an amazing young woman, and I can't wait to see what her unique perspective brings to this complicated world.

I would like to give an enormous *grazie mille* to Professor Mario Primicerio for his two years of correspondence, in which he shared with me events in his personal life and his thoughts on politics, not only in Italy but in the United States as well. His dedication and hard work as a professor, as the president of the Fondazione Giorgio La Pira, and as a loving family man are inspiring.

As with any research endeavor, there are bound to be stones left unturned. The global 2020 pandemic caused setbacks in some areas of my research. The archives for the Center for the Study of Democratic Institutions that are stored on the campus of UC, Santa Barbara contain two boxes labeled "Giorgio La Pira." When the restrictions surrounding the pandemic are lifted, I'm hoping that my daughter and I can take a peek inside. Who knows—maybe our journey will continue.

Ryan McAnany

Appendix

Biographical Factsheet of a Servant of God
Giorgio La Pira
9 January 1904–5 November 1977

Fondazione Giorgio La Pira
Florence

"There is no doubt that the Lord instilled the desire for priestly grace into my soul. Only, He wants me to continue donning my lay apparel so that my work be more fecund in the secular world that is far from Him. But the aim of my life is clearly set forth which is to be a missionary of the Lord in the world, and I must carry out this apostolate in the conditions and the setting within which the Lord has set me."

Giorgio La Pira
April 1931
From the letter to his aunt Settimia Occhipinti

"One last thing: I am not a priest as you thought: Jesus did not wish this of me! I am only a young man to whom Jesus has given a great blessing, namely a boundless desire to love him and for him to be boundlessly loved."

Giorgio La Pira
Easter 1933
From the letter to the Mother Prioress
of the convent of S. Maria Maddalena de'Pazzi

1904: He was born on 9 January in Pozzallo (province of Ragusa) to Gaetano La Pira and Angela Occhipinti, the first of six children.

He was baptized on 7 February in Madonna del Rosario, the Mother Church of Pozzallo. His uncle Luigi Occhipinti, his mother's brother, stood as godfather.

1909–1913: He attended the Giacinto Pandolfi Primary School in Pozzallo up to fourth year.

He then moved to Messina to stay with his uncle Luigi Occhipinti where he completed his primary education and continued his studies.

1914–1917: He attended the Antonello Technical-Commercial College up to third year.

1917: He attended the A. M. Jaci Technical-Commercial College and graduated in accounting and commerce.

At this time he met and associated with a group of adolescents that included Salvatore Quasimodo, future Nobel laureate for literature and Salvatore Pugliatti, future Dean of Messina University.

1921: He worked in his uncle Luigi Occhipinti's company, in order to contribute toward keeping himself at school.

1922: He studied for his Classic High School final exam in a single school year and obtained his diploma in Palermo. During that year he often visited the home of Federico Rampolla (his Italian teacher at the "Jaci") who helped him prepare for the high school final exam in Latin and Greek. This is where he met Federico's brother, the priest Fr. Mariano Rampolla. A strong bond of friendship grew between the two which was to be of great help to La Pira in terms of spirituality and culture and which continued in the years when both were in Rome.

With his high school diploma, he enrolled in the school of law at Messina University with Prof. Emilio Betti, who took the young La Pira under his wing. He continued law for three academic years until 1925 when Prof. Betti moved to Florence and invited La Pira to join him. In Florence, La Pira studied the fourth academic year of law.

1924: Easter was a time of special grace for La Pira, as he himself wrote: "I will never forget that Easter of 1924 when I received Christ through the Eucharist; I felt an innocence so full flowing through my veins that

I could not stop myself from singing and feeling incommensurable happiness."

1925: He became a Dominican Tertiary, taking the name of Frà Raimondo in the first group of tertiaries founded by Fr. Enrico Di Vita in Messina.

1926: He passed his last two final exams (forensic medicine and administrative law), graduating summa cum laude on 10 July with the right to publish his thesis. This, entitled "Intestate and counter-testate hereditary succession in Roman law," published under the auspices of the University of Florence by Vallecchi, Florence, 1930, was dedicated by La Pira "To Contardo Ferrini who by every path restored me to the House of the Lord."

That same year, on a recommendation by Prof. Betti, the University of Florence appointed him lecturer in Roman law. In the 1926–27 academic year he led a course of fifteen lectures on Roman hereditary law.

1927: He competed for a scholarship to specialize in Roman law in both Italy and abroad. He won both scholarships and decided to study abroad. At the same time, the University of Florence confirmed his appointment as lecturer in Roman law which he had to decline after a short introduction of fifteen lessons because of his imminent departure for Austria and Germany for his scholarship.

At the Universities of Vienna and Munich he attended lessons by Professors Wlassak, Woess and Wenger, gleaning a lot of new material for his own further studies.

He returned to Italy in November and the "Cesare Alfieri" Social Science department of the University of Florence appointed him lecturer in Roman law for the academic year 1928–29.

On 11 December he donned the habit of a Dominican Tertiary in the Basilica of San Marco under the name of Frà Raimondo.

1928: In June, the University of Florence appointed him lecturer of the history of Greek-Roman law for the 1929–30 academic year. This took the shape of a monographic course on some aspects of the Papyrus Laws.

He became a member of the Institute for Kingship, which he had contributed to establishing. The statute of the "The Secular Institute of Missionaries of the Kingship of Christ" describes it as "a community of laymen established and governed in accordance with the Constitution of the 'Provvida Mater Ecclesia' and the 'Primo feliciter' Motu Proprio for special consecration to God in the service of mankind." Pursuant to this membership, the adherent takes a vow of poverty, obedience and celibacy in chastity. The Institute is part of the great spiritual movement of Franciscan Tertiaries of which it shares objectives and ideals. St. Francis of Assisi—and his plan and message of "peace and all good"—is thus an essential and constant guiding light in La Pira's life.

1930: On 31 March he qualified for university professorship in Roman law.

1933: Aged 29, he was appointed full professor of Roman law.

He was active in the Florence section of Catholic Action and carried out his apostolate mission in the "problem" areas around Empoli.

La Pira held Cardinal Elia Dalla Costa, Archbishop of Florence, in especially high regard, a consideration that was amply reciprocated. There were long periods when he visited the cardinal every evening to exchange views and opinions on current affairs as they unfolded in Florence and the rest of the world, and it was Cardinal Dalla Costa who inspired La Pira's profound enjoyment of the Bible as the only book for interpreting the history of today.

Around this time he met Fr. Giulio Facibeni, a charismatic figure in the Florence church, priest of Rifredi and founder of the Opera Madonnina del Grappa. The pair struck up a firm bond of friendship that was to have positive repercussions on the city itself. They shared joy and pain, suffering and hope.

Florentines used to say that the city had three saints: Cardinal Dalla Costa (faith), La Pira (hope), and Fr. Facibeni (charity). And there is surely some significance in all three being in the process of beatification.

1934: In this period he met Mons. Giovanni Battista Montini and the two remained firm friends all their lives. Indeed it was Mons. Montini who pointed La Pira to Mons. Raffaele Bensi, who became his spiritual mentor, confessor and friend.

Inspired by one of Don Bensi's observations on the abject poverty of the city, La Pira founded the "Mass of San Procolo" to provide spiritual and material assistance to the poor. He convinced a great number of the city's young people from different economic backgrounds to cooperate in the initiative. The magistrate Renzo Poggi was also an activist.

1935: On 3 June, he set up the Vincentian Conference entitled "San Bernardino da Siena" to provide assistance to writers, artists and craftsmen. The Conference was composed almost exclusively of writers and artists including Carlo Bo, Piero Bargellini, Nicola Lisi, Giovanni Papini and Pietro Parigi.

1936: He entered San Marco's Dominican community and was assigned cell number 6, "full of light and silent, but cold and unadorned," as Fr. Cipriano Ricotti later wrote.

During his stay in the monastery he furthered his studies on the works of St. Thomas Aquinas, which contributed to the formation of his philosophy and Christian mentality.

1937: He set up a second Vincentian Conference, this time entitled "Beato Angelico," prevalently composed of magistrates and lawyers who met at the Editrice Fiorentina bookshop owned by the brothers Vittorio and Valerio Zani.

1939: He officially became "Donato", a Dominican in the monastery of San Marco.

He was the founder and editor of *Principi* (*Principles*), an anti-fascist periodical that defended freedom and the worth of the human being. The following year, fascists forced the magazine to close down. La Pira became a wanted man and was forced into hiding.

1943: After 29 September, the day when Nazi-Fascists ransacked the Monastery of San Marco hunting for him and Fr. Coiro, he sought refuge with the Mazzei family in Fonterutoli in the province of Siena. The Fascist police traced him there, too, and La Pira was obliged to hide in Trefole, a nearby outlying district where the cold and damp gave him severe bronchitis. In the three months he stayed in Fonterutoli his friendship with Fioretta Mazzei developed and grew. This was a close, very profound relationship based on a communion of thought, intentions and spirituality.

On 17 November a warrant for La Pira's arrest was served on the Monastery of San Marco. On hearing of this in Fonterutoli from Fr. Cipriano Ricotti, he declared, "I have never hated or killed anyone. In You, oh Lord, *speravi non confundar in aeternum* [I place my trust, let me never be put to shame]." He eventually left the area of Fonterutoli on 8 December in the company of his friend Pollicina, an engineer and manager of the Florence gas company, and after an adventuresome journey took refuge in Rome. Pollicina was killed during an air raid which La Pira survived despite being nearby.

On 30 September the Governorship of Vatican City issued La Pira with nominative ID N° 4858 as a staff member of the newspaper *L'Osservatore Romano*. He changed homes frequently during his stay in Rome: he stayed with the Pollicinas, with the Rampollas, with Ms. Panicci (where he wrote the life story of Fr. Moresco), then in the S. Uffizio and lastly with Monsignor Montini.

1944: In September he went back to Florence, which had just been liberated, and to the Monastery of San Marco, but then frequent bouts of bronchitis forced him to abandon his cold cell in San Marco's and live in a room in the clinic owned by his friend Prof. Palumbo in Via Venezia. Here, he was lovingly cared for by the Sisters of the Misericordia for more than twenty-five years.

He was appointed President of the Municipal Assistance Organisation where he was active in providing assistance to people reduced to poverty because of the war. He appointed Fr. Raffaele Bensi as his assistant and selected as his secretary Antinesca Rabissi, who was to follow him faithfully until his death.

1946: He was elected deputy to the Constituent Assembly, and together with such figures as Moro, Dossetti, Basso, Calamandrei and Togliatti, he drafted the founding principles of the Constitution of the Republic establishing civil and religious rights, the right to employment and the value of the human person. He made a decisive contribution to Article 7—on the relationship between Church and State—and for getting it approved.

1948: In the general election he was elected to the Chamber of Deputies and appointed Undersecretary of

State for Labour under De Gasperi. He won respect by his support for workers in the serious trade union negotiations in post-war Italy.

In this period he was developing an interest in politics as a part of life together with his friends Giuseppe Dossetti, Amintore Fanfani and Giuseppe Lazzati with whom he established the periodical *Cronache Sociali* (*Social Chronicles*), in which he published a series of important articles, the most renowned of which was "*L'attesa della povera gente* [The expectation of poor people]."

Two years later, disagreement on the economy and reforms led him and other members of the Dossetti group to resign from the government. During his tenure at the Ministry of Labour he appointed as his secretary his close friend from St. Procolo, Dr. Enzo Sarti, who unfortunately died young.

1951: He asked Togliatti, who was leaving for Moscow, to urge Stalin toward a political solution to the Korean War.

Despite serious misgivings, La Pira gave in to the pressure he was being subjected to from all quarters, including the Church, and stood as the leading candidate for the Christian Democrat Party in the local elections of 10 and 11 June. He agreed on condition of his project being accepted for giving a concrete, all-encompassing response to the new political emergencies, a project very close to his heart, especially after his experience in government following the constitutional assembly. The four-party coalition he led won the election and on 5 July La Pira was elected as mayor of Florence, taking the place of

Mario Fabiani, who had headed a left-wing administration in the four previous years.

As President of the High Commission of Tuscany for the Conference of St. Vincent, he began a correspondence with all the cloistered women's convents and, jointly with the Ministry of the Interior, began sending them financial aid to help them over the period of great distress caused by the war.

1952: In the height of the "cold war" he launched the Conferences for Christian Peace and Civilisation which in its five sessions was officially attended by many countries including the Holy See, as well as by many notable intellectuals, both Christian and non-Christian.

1953: "Cities not homes": Faced with the severe housing crisis caused by evictions, war damage and the influx of flood victims from the low lying Polesine coastal area in Italy's north east, La Pira built hundreds of "minimal houses" to deal with the most acute emergencies and completed the construction of the large new neighbourhood of Isolotto, which provided good-quality, stable housing to thousands of people.

He took part in the movement to save 2000 blue-collar jobs in Pignone and through the intervention of the president of the holding company ENI, Enrico Mattei (with whom he was friendly), he contributed to saving the company. The skill on the part of La Pira and Mattei opened up the international marketplace to "Nuovo Pignone."

Every Saturday he visited prisoners, and through the offices of his friend Giampaolo Meucci, the magistrate, he assisted them in their court cases.

1954: He requisitioned the Cure foundry which was being liquidated by its owners and transformed it into a cooperative partnership.

Shocked by the devastation wreaked by nuclear weapons, he spoke at the headquarters of the International Red Cross in Geneva on the value of cities and asked, "Do states have the right to destroy cities?"

1955: Every Christmas and Easter of these years he sent letters to the children attending primary and middle schools, to the sick and to grandparents about the "vocation" of their city and to explain the achievements of the city government and its political orientation.

The echoes produced by his speech in Geneva led him to organize the Convention of Mayors of the World's Capital Cities. For the first time, mayors of the Western world met with their counterparts from the East; they talked and signed a pact of peace. The mayor of Moscow raised some eyebrows by attending High Mass celebrated by Cardinal Elia Dalla Costa in the Franciscan Basilica of Santa Croce.

During this term in office, La Pira was active in organizing twinning with certain important cities such as Rheims and Fez with the aim of creating a system of bridges as a means for constructing unity among peoples.

At this time, the city government also reconstructed the Grazie and Santa Trinita bridges and built the new

Vespucci Bridge. In addition, the Central Dairy, the new Municipal Theatre and the fruit and vegetable market in Novoli were completed and the city tramway, cleaning service and waterworks were modernized.

1956: Local elections took place on 27–28 May. The Christian Democrats headed by La Pira increased their share of the vote from 36.24% to 39.29%. The Communist Party polled 12,600 votes fewer than 1951. La Pira enjoyed a resounding personal success with 33,907 preferences against 19,192 of 1951.

Paradoxically, however, the new electoral law being rigidly proportional made it harder to form a majority, which was not made any easier by the political situation at the national level. However, he was re-elected mayor of Florence on the third vote.

On 15 May, La Pira went to Venice for a conference and was invited to dinner by the Patriarch Mons. Angelo Roncalli. The evening sped by in amicable conversation and, realizing it had grown late, Cardinal Roncalli gave hospitality to La Pira in the patriarchate; in great secret, though, he had him sleep in the bed that had belonged to Pius X.

On the evening of 6 November 1983 during his stay in Florence, Mons. Loris Capovilla, secretary to John XXIII, revealed that the then-Patriarch had made the following entry in his daily diary: "I spent yesterday evening with Prof. La Pira whom I esteem and venerate. His is a soul worthy of all respect."

1957: On 17 June La Pira realized he could no longer continue for lack of a majority to approve the city budget. He therefore resigned and with him the whole city council; the prefect appointed a commissioner to administer the city the same day.

Despite this, he carried out the prior engagement in Florence with King Mohammed V of Morocco, namely to summon all the Mediterranean peoples to Palazzo Vecchio in Florence to foster—*spes contra spem*, hope against hope—pacification and unity among them.

To this end he went on a pilgrimage to Israel, Jordan and Egypt, and also travelled extensively to Paris, Rabat, Tunis and Beirut.

On 17 September, on the day of celebration of the Stigmata, he accompanied Prince Moulay Abdallah, the son of King Mohammed V, to the Sanctuary of La Verna to repay the visit that St. Francis had paid to the Sultan of Egypt and to commemorate St. Francis's two attempts to meet the Sultan of Morocco.

1958: La Pira stood as the Christian Democrat leading candidate in the general election and won a seat in the Chamber of Deputies.

He stood alongside the whole city in defending the Officine Galileo and he drafted a bill for employment contracts to recognize *erga omnes*, the right of all to work.

In October, he held the first "Conversations for the Mediterranean." For the first time Arabs and Israelis, French and Algerians, represented by men of culture and, albeit in a personal capacity, by personalities with institutional positions, sat around the same table to talk about the issues that divided their peoples.

It could be said that the Evian Agreement (1962) that gave Algeria its independence had its prologue in Florence. The idea behind this initiative was to create an area of peace among all the nations bordering on the Mediterranean—"Tiberius' Great Lake"—and to unite the peoples of the three-fold family of Abraham: Jews, Christians and Muslims.

1959: Invited to the USSR, he went to Moscow with his friend, the journalist Vittorio Citterich, and spoke to members of the Supreme Soviet in defense of détente and disarmament. He also met the most representative intellectuals and talked about the issue of the atheism of the State. Before setting out for Moscow, he went to Fatima to pray to the Madonna for protection and he wrote to the women of cloistered convents for them to accompany him with their prayers.

1960: On 24 January, on his way back from Cairo he made a stopover in Istanbul where he met the Patriarch Athenagoras of Constantinople. The conversation focused on the unity of the Church as an inevitable phase toward the unity of peoples and of nations. Patriarch Athenagoras gave La Pira a box of sweetmeats to give to Pope John XXIII.

1960–1964: He was again the leading candidate for the Christian Democrats in the local election held on 6–7 November 1960 for the city council, in which he won a resounding personal success.

After lengthy inter-party negotiations, on the first of March 1961, La Pira was appointed mayor for the third time to lead one of the first center-left city governments. For the second time he abandoned national politics to serve the city of Florence.

At this time a number of large-scale public works were brought to completion and the new town-planning program was defined, which saved Florence from speculative building. In only three years, 17 new schools were built, as was the Affrico flyover and the covering of the brook of the same name, the major underground passageways under the station square, the repair of over 90 private roads, and then providing a roof for the homeless was continued.

In addition, La Pira produced a series of initiatives of great political, cultural and social worth. He proposed that a European university be built in Florence; he gave his support to the emergence of new African States and invited Léopold Sédar Senghor, poet and writer, to Florence. As well as being one of the leaders of the African liberation movement, Senghor was also the president of the Republic of Senegal. La Pira went to the United Sates to give his support to laws granting civil rights to minority groups. He gave impetus to Florence twinning with Philadelphia and Kiev. He continued struggling for peace and unity among peoples and in these years he convened the second, third and fourth Mediterranean Conversations. He also invited the plenary session of the International Committee for Space Research to meet in Florence.

He gave honorary citizenship of Florence to UN Secretary General U Thant; Le Corbusier, the great urban architect; and Pablo Casals, one of the symbols of opposition to the Franco regime in Spain.

He convened the ninth session of the East-West Round Table on Disarmament in Florence. He received Ajubei and the daughter of Khrushchev in Palazzo Vecchio, accompanied by the USSR Ambassador to Italy Kozirev. Ajubei and his wife were later received by the pope in Rome. He organized preparatory conferences for the great event of the Second Vatican Council, calling on great theologians of the caliber of J. Danielou, H. Férét, Y. Congar and E. Balducci. Participation in these conferences was massive.

Local city council elections took place on 22–23 November 1964 and La Pira was again the main candidate for the Christian Democrat Party. Again he won a resounding personal victory but the political climate had deteriorated through conflict between currents within the majority party itself and he was obliged to withdraw his candidacy for mayor.

1965: In March he left the office of mayor of Florence for the last time.

This did not stop him seeking a political solution to the war in Vietnam. In close cooperation with Amintore Fanfani, then Italy's Minister for Foreign Affairs, and with the Polish Ambassador to Italy Wilmann, he went to London where he met with Labour MPs to organize an International Symposium for Peace in Vietnam. The symposium was held in April in the Forte di Belvedere, and was attended by parliamentarians and politicians from Britain, France, USSR and Italy, as well as by representatives of international bodies. It ended with an appeal signed by La Pira and Lord Fenner Brockway, which was sent to the governments that signed the 1954 Geneva agreements on Vietnam and to those involved in the conflict.

The appeal was answered by Ho Chi Minh, President of the Republic of North Vietnam, specifying the points indispensable for the restoration of peace. After a period of painstaking preparation, La Pira was given the substantial go-ahead by all the parties involved in the conflict and so, in October, he left for Hanoi together with Prof. Mario Primicerio, by way of Warsaw, Moscow and Beijing. On 11 November he met President Ho Chi Minh and Prime Minister Pham Van Dong.

He came back to Italy with a peace proposal which he handed officially to the President of the UN General Assembly, Amintore Fanfani. The initiative was sabotaged by leaks to the American press and peace was only achieved eight years later, on the same conditions that were offered by the La Pira mission but at the cost of immense destruction and hundreds of thousands of lives.

1966: He took an active part in addressing the problems caused by the flooding in Florence. He helped the city by drawing on his international relations and he was invited to fundraising initiatives in Paris, New York, Montreal and Ottawa.

In the preface of the book *Thou Shalt not Kill*, edited by Fabrizio Fabbrini, he reviewed and healed the deep disagreement that had developed around conscientious objection, which had put Florence under the limelight nationwide. This had stemmed from a series of events including a private screening of Claude Autant-Lara's film *Tu ne tueras point [Thou shalt not kill]* (1961), the sentence handed down to conscientious objector Giuseppe Gozzini (1962) and the trials of Fr. Ernesto Balducci (1963) and Fr. Lorenzo Milani (1965).

1967: He was elected President of the World Federation of United Cities (FMCU) with headquarters in Paris. The organization, recognized by the UN, coined the slogan "Unite the cities to unite the world." La Pira viewed the Federation as an additional complementary face of the United Nations.

The "Six-Day War" that broke out between Israel and bordering Arab States brought the issue of peace in the Middle East dramatically to center stage, highlighting the growing autonomy and importance on the international political stage of the Palestinian movements grouped together under the PLO.

Between Christmas 1967 and Epiphany 1968 he repeated his pilgrim's odyssey of ten years earlier with the same objective—peace and dialogue. Together with Giorgio Giovannoni he travelled first to Israel and then to Egypt, holding lengthy talks with Israeli Foreign Minister Abba Eban and President of Egypt Nasser and with the mayors of Hebron and Bethlehem as well as with Palestinian representatives of East Jerusalem in the occupied West Bank.

1968: He took part in the Tunis World Conference of the FMCU youth movement and made a speech on the protest movement, affirming: "Young people are like swallows—they fly towards the Spring."

This was the year of youth protests. He followed the actions of the student movement very closely. He was one of the few professors of the University of Florence who was not heckled. He went to Paris frequently to speak to gatherings of young people in the Sorbonne together with the film director Roberto Rossellini.

As President of the FMCU he was invited by the mayor of Prague to follow the development of the events of the "Prague Spring." He held several meetings including a highly significant one with Minister of Foreign Affairs Hayeck.

1969–1970: In these years, La Pira led the cities within the FMCU to be active in the process of East-West détente launched with Willy Brandt's Ostpolitik; in Helsinki, Stockholm, East Berlin, Budapest, Vienna and Potsdam. He tackled the issue of the *de jure* recognition of the German Democratic Republic and of European nuclear disarmament as a means toward détente, peace and unity within the continent of Europe, encouraging cities and nations to work towards a pan-European conference.

He was frequently in Paris, again in Stockholm, Helsinki and Moscow, where he had frequent contacts with the Vietnamese delegation in an attempt to speed up the inauguration of the Paris Conference for Peace in Vietnam. In Jerusalem, Tel Aviv, Bethlehem and Hebron, he publicly espoused the "triangular theory" (Israel, Palestine, Arab

States) on which to base the real negotiations for peace in the Middle East.

An FMCU conference was held in Leningrad in which the system of bridges linking cities became more concrete. La Pira proposed a new system of town twinning, namely cooperative twinning between cities in the East, the West and the South.

In 1968 a serious crisis hit the Florence Church— the case of Isolotto and Fr. Mazzi. In the most serious moment of this crisis, on 3 September 1969, La Pira made a clear choice and sided with the city's bishop Cardinal Florit. By publicly stating "*Ubi Petrus et episcopus ibi Ecclesia* [The Church is where Peter and the Bishop are]," La Pira redefined the Isolotto question—similarly to all his decisions, it gave priority to fidelity to and unity of the Church over personal feelings, no matter how much suffering this may cause.

La Pira's stance in the Isolotto case, which met with criticism from many of his friends, was given great importance in the declaration that Cardinal Florit issued on La Pira's death: "It is no wonder that a man of this kind could also make the unpopular choice he made nine years ago when the Church in Florence and its bishop had to suffer great pain. He was close to me then as a brother and that was of great help to me in carrying out a painful and tiresome duty."

1970: The Palumbo clinic in Via Venezia closed down and La Pira moved to the premises of the Opera per la Gioventù founded by Pino Arpioni, who had

worked with him in the city council and who had dedicated his life to giving a Christian upbringing to young
people. Proximity to young people made the last years of
La Pira's life happier and more complete.

Next door to the Opera were the premises of "Cultura,"
a center of political and cultural activism managed by
Gianni and Giorgio Giovannoni, who had also published
many of La Pira's written works. Here, too, the presence of
La Pira was constant and constructive.

1971–1973: These years saw the perfection of the "conferences of convergence" on which he had spent so much
effort in the previous six years. In July 1973 the Conference
on Security and Cooperation in Europe (CSCE) was held
in Helsinki; in Paris there was the conference on the end
of the war and peacekeeping in Vietnam; the UN held a
conference in Geneva on a Middle East ceasefire after the
fourth Arab-Israeli war (1973).

La Pira continued to work tirelessly toward these
objectives, travelling extensively to Moscow, Warsaw, Bonn,
Berlin, Budapest, Sofia, for Europe; to Cairo, Jerusalem,
and Beirut for the Middle East; to New York and Quebec
(Canada) for Vietnam.

He also went to Chile in an attempt to head off the
coup d'état threatening the democratic socialist government of President Salvador Allende.

In Houston, Texas, he took part in a seminar organized
by the de Menyll Foundation, attended by world figures of
culture and science including a number of Nobel laureates
summoned to debate "Plans for the Future."

In Zagorsk, USSR, La Pira met the Patriarch of the Russian Orthodox Church Pimen and the head of the Department for Foreign Affairs Nikodim, to talk about unity among Christian Churches.

In December 1973 he went to Dakar where he concluded his FMCU presidency and was reconfirmed as president for a third term.

1974–1975: He was invited to Paris for the closing ceremony of the Vietnam peace negotiations.

While following the ups and downs of the "conferences on convergence" from Paris and Florence, he dedicated much effort to Italian politics, taking an active part in the campaign for the referendum on divorce and viewing with growing alarm the destabilizing effect caused by post-fascist terrorism and the first stirrings of the Red Brigades.

At the conclusion of the Helsinki Conference (August 1975) he was invited by UNESCO to a conference in October where he drafted the new navigational map for the peoples of Europe (enshrined by the signatures of the heads of government in the final Act of Helsinki).

1976: He took a high profile in the battle against abortion, tackling the issue not only from a religious but also a civil standpoint. On 19 March 1976, the Vatican daily *L'Osservatore Romano* gave front-page coverage to his article of great cultural and religious depth entitled "Di fronte all'aborto [Faced with Abortion]."

The political situation in Italy was serious. Protests, scandals and terrorism were undermining the country's democratic institutions. The Christian Democrat national secretary Benigno Zaccagnini again put La Pira under pressure to run as the party's main candidate in Florence in the general elections. Despite health problems, La Pira accepted in order to continue in his struggle for disarmament, unity and peace and to affirm the primacy of human and Christian values in an increasingly violent and materialistic society.

He was elected to the Chamber of Deputies with a landslide of preference votes and also to the Senate for the constituency of Montevarchi. He opted for the Chamber of Deputies.

1977: On Saturday 5 November La Pira passed away in the Clinic of the English Sisters in via Cherubini in Florence ". . . in the Sabbath without vespers on which the sun never sets."

Shortly beforehand he had received a handwritten letter from Pope Paul VI, which for him was the last great source of joy—the final act by the Church that he had loved so much.

The first blessing of the body was given by Cardinal Giovanni Benelli, Archbishop of Florence, in the room where La Pira had lain since a few minutes after his death. That night, Holy Mass was celebrated in the same room by Fr. Giuseppe Dossetti in the presence of family and close friends.

The body of La Pira lay in state in the Badia Fiorentina for the Mass of San Procolo and then in the Church of San Marco from 6 November until the funeral the following day. A never-ending procession of members of the public, friends, and personalities of every political and religious creed came from all over Italy and abroad to pay their respects to La Pira, whom everyone now called the "*Sindaco Santo* [Saint Mayor]."

The funeral cortège wended its way through the most significant places of La Pira's career, escorted by a massive crowd: the Church of San Marco; the university, where the dean, Prof. Ferroni, commemorated his merits as a scholar and teacher before a throng of his colleagues; then Piazza Santissima Annunziata where, in front of the Marian Basilica so close to La Pira's heart, Fr. Davide Maria Turoldo said a prayer and took leave of his great friend for the last time; San Michelino Visdomini, where thousands of times La Pira had climbed the famous "Don Bensi Staircase," to visit his spiritual guide and confessor and where Don Bensi himself, who more than anyone knew his soul, gave the body the last blessing; to the Badia Fiorentina, a tangible sign of his fidelity to the poorest, where he received the blessing of Mons. Bonanni and his friends of San Procolo; Piazza della Signoria, in front of Palazzo Vecchio, for many years the focus of his thoughts and his political and administrative work, where before a crowd of thousands, the heads of the state institutions, the standards of many cities and family and friends, he was officially commemorated by the city and civil society with speeches by Mayor Elio Gabbuggiani, Senator Amintore Fanfani and Prof. Giuseppe Lazzati. The Maggio Musicale Fiorentino Orchestra accompanied the cortège towards the Cathedral.

In Piazza della Signoria, the seat of civil power, the body was passed to the religious cortège composed of hundreds of priests who accompanied it to Santa Maria del Fiore, the religious center of the city, where Cardinal Giovanni Benelli celebrated the funeral Mass and exalted the religious aspects of the life of Giorgio La Pira.

During the Angelus in Piazza San Pietro on Sunday 6 November, he was commemorated by Pope Paul VI.

The body of Giorgio La Pira was laid to rest in the Florence cemetery of Rifredi next to Fr. Giulio Facibeni, a place for thought and prayer for many. His tomb is adorned by a lamp gifted by youths from Florence, Israel and Palestine that bears the inscription "Pace, shalom, salaam."

1986: On 9 January, the 82nd anniversary of La Pira's birth, Cardinal Silvano Piovanelli, Archbishop of Florence, opened the diocesan process for his beatification in the Dominican Basilica of San Marco.

"La Pira's little coffin was shouldered by the people of Florence as they had shouldered those of Fr. Giulio Facibeni and Cardinal Elia Dalla Costa. Without their realizing it, the humble and the unlearned were the link for three personages: a priest, a cardinal and a mayor, all three wholly dispossessed of worldly goods and all three empowered to take the *todo y nada* of St. John of the Cross: 'To have everything possess nothing of nothing. To be everything be nothing of nothing.'"

Mons. Loris F. Capovilla

Endnotes

1. Pope John Paul II, "Address to the Members of the National Association of Italian Communes (ANCI)," April 26, 2004, https://www.vatican.va/content/john-paul-ii/en/speeches/2004/april/documents/hf_jp-ii_spe_20040426_anci.html.

2. Giorgio La Pira, in a speech on the historical prospect of the progressive unity of the world. Given at the inaugural session of the International Youth Conference for Peace and Disarmament, February 1964.

3. "1943," "Giorgio La Pira, Servant of God: A Biographical Time-Line," Florin, accessed October 7, 2020, http://www.florin.ms/giorgiopira.html.

4. James Hershberg, *Marigold: The Lost Chance for Peace in Vietnam* (Stanford: Stanford University Press, 2012), 16–22.

5. Mario Primicerio, *Con La Pira in Viet Nam* (Florence: Edizioni Polistampa, 2016).

6. "#Soul, Mario Primicerio ospite di Monica Mondo," Tv2000it, March 16, 2019, https://www.youtube.com/watch?v=NhleY2XaprQ&t=67.

7. Mario Primicerio, email to author, June 28, 2019.

8. David Kraslow and Stuart H. Loory, *The Secret Search for Peace in Vietnam* (Random House, 1968).

9. "From the Association to the Foundation," Fondazione Giorgio La Pira, accessed June 11, 2021, https://www.fondazionelapira.org/dalla-associazione-alla-fondazione/.

10. Associated Press, "Italy Swept By New Riots; 150 Arrested," *Oakland [CA] Tribune*, May 25, 1949, D3, available at Newspapers.com.

11. Associated Press, "Italy Farm Strike Settled," *Salt Lake Telegram*, June 24, 1949, 2, available at Newspapers.com.

12. Associated Press, "Italy's Farm Strike Ends," *Scranton [PA] Times-Tribune*, June 24, 1949, 5, available at Newspapers.com.
13. Paul McC. Warner, "Today Italians and ERP Opinions Differ Called Aid to Rich Poverty Oppressive People Must Be Told," *Philadelphia Inquirer*, May 18, 1950, 1, 23, available at Newspapers.com.
14. George Bria. "Red Mayor Of Florence Won't Scare Tourist," *Bangor [ME] Daily News*, July 14, 1947, 15, available at Newspapers.com.
15. Associated Press, "City of Florence Gives Welcome To Friendship Train," *Santa Cruz [CA] Sentinel*, January 2, 1948, 3, available at Newspapers.com.
16. Associated Press, "270-Car Friendship ship Train Gets New York Welcome," *Glen Falls [NY] Post-Star*, November 19, 1947, 1, available at Newspapers.com.
17. McC. Warner, "Today Italians and ERP Opinions Differ."
18. Jack Brusini, "Life Abroad-37: Italy's Poorest Man, Mayor Of Richest City," *Long Branch [NJ] Daily Record*, August 18, 1951, 3, available at Newspapers.com.
19. Associated Press, "Monastic Educator Is Likely Mayor," *Tucson Daily Citizen*, June 14, 1951, 21, available at Newspapers.com.
20. Associated Press, "Defeat of Reds Stinging Event," *Spokane [WA] Chronicle*, June 2, 1952, 14, available at Newspapers.com.
21. Jack Brusini, "Italy's Richest City Honors Poorest Man," *Bergen [Hackensack, NJ] Evening Record*, August 18, 1951, 9, available at Newspapers.com.
22. Ibid.
23. Ibid.
24. Ibid.
25. Jack Brusini, "Town's Poorest Man Becomes Mayor Of Italy's Richest City: Florence's Chief Lives In Convent Cell, Helps Poor, Even Aids Communistic Foes," *Passaic [NJ] Herald-News*, August 18, 1951, 9, available at Newspapers.com.
26. Jack Brusini, "City Of Flowers is Ruled By Italy's Poorest Citizen," *Binghamton [NY] Press and Sun-Bulletin*, August 18, 1951, 2, available at Newspapers.com.
27. Jack Brusini, "Humble Disciple Of Poverty Mayor of Italy's Richest City," *Central New Jersey Home News*, August 18, 1951, 3, available at Newspapers.com.
28. Brusini, "Life Abroad-37: Italy's Poorest Man, Mayor Of Richest City."
29. Associated Press, "Poorest Man Heads Richest City of Italy," *Sioux Falls [SD] Argus-Leader*, August 19, 1951, 31, available at Newspapers.com.
30. Jack Brusini, "Mayor of Italy's Richest City Has Poverty as Creed," *Cedar Rapids [IA] Gazette*, August 19, 1951, 13, available at Newspapers.com.

31. Associated Press, "Mayor Of Fabulous Florence Is The Poorest Man In Italy," *Beatrice [NE] Daily Sun*, August 24, 1951, 2, available at Newspapers.com.

32. The Editors of Encyclopaedia Britannica, "Anne Elizabeth O'Hare Mc-Cormick: American journalist," Encyclopaedia Britannica, last updated May 25, 2021, https://www.britannica.com/biography/Anne-Elizabeth-OHare-McCormick.

33. Anne O'Hare McCormick, "Abroad: A Portrait of the Mayor of Florence," *New York Times*, December 12, 1951, 36, available at TimesMachine, timesmachine.nytimes.com.

34. Ibid.

35. Ibid.

36. Ibid.

37. Giorgio La Pira, "A letter to his Aunt and Uncle in 1926: La Pira stated his love for Florence," https://www.fondazionelapira.org/.

38. Special to the New York Times, "Arnaldo Cortesi Is Dead at 69: Times Foreign Correspondent," *New York Times*, November 27, 1966, 86, available at TimesMachine, timesmachine.nytimes.com.

39. Arnaldo Cortesi, "Florentines Battle Architecture Smear," *Atlanta [GA] Constitution*, February 25, 1952, 8, available at Newspapers.com.

40. Ibid.

41. Reuters, "Urbino Vs Florence -Dispute over Famed Work of Raphael May Be Ended," *Fort Worth Star-Telegram*, November 8, 1956, 51, available at Newspapers.com.

42. Ibid.

43. Giulio Andreotti, "The answer to the anxieties of an era," Formiche.net, June 1, 2011.

44. Roberto Bonuglia, "Il Codice di Camldoli e la 'ricostruzione' cattolica" ("The Camaldoli Code and the Catholic 'reconstruction'"), Fondazione Cristoforo Colombo per le libertà, December 12, 2013, accessed June 9, 2021, https://web.archive.org/web/20140203132845/http://www2.cara-vella.eu/wp-content/uploads/2011/12/Diario-di-Bordo-n-14-Il-Codice-di-Camaldoli-.pdf.

45. Techdecisions. "Nov 5 – Servant of God Giorgio La Pira (1904-1977), The Godly Mayor – A Job, a House, & Music…," Adult Catechesis and Christian Religious Literacy, November 2, 2012, https://soul-candy.info/2012/11/nov-5-servant-of-god-giorgio-la-pira-1904-1977-the-god-ly-mayor-a-job-a-house-music/.

46. Roberto Di Ferdinando, "La Pira, Mattei and the saving of Pignone's jobs in Florence," November 12, 2019, ScenariEconomici, https://scenarieco-nomici.it/la-pira-mattei-e-il-salvataggio-dei-posti-di-lavoro-del-pignone-a-firenze/.

47. National Catholic Welfare Council News Service, "Reveals Pope Had Role in Sit-Down Strike," *Brooklyn [NY] Tablet*, December 12, 1953, 21, available at Newspapers.com.

48. "ITALY: The Saint and the Unemployed," *Time Magazine*, December 7, 1953, The TIME Vault, http://content.time.com/time/subscriber/article/0,33009,890726,00.html.

49. National Catholic Welfare Council News Service, "Reveals Pope Had Role in Sit-Down Strike."

50. Di Ferdinando, "La Pira, Mattei and the saving of Pignone's jobs in Florence."

51. "A Lesson from Abroad," *Troy [NY] Times Record*, December 24, 1953, 16, available at Newspapers.com.

52. Marquis W. Childs, "Real Danger of Communist Hold on Italy Is Difficult to Evaluate: Odd
Conflicts and Alliances, Feudalism and Church Contribute to Problem Which Officials Say Americans Overemphasize," *St. Louis [MO] Dispatch*, April 25, 1954, 28, available at Newspapers.com.

53. Ibid.

54. Ibid.

55. Ibid.

56. Associated Press, "Italian Mayor Seizes Foundry, Turns Firm Over to Workers," *Baltimore Evening Sun*, February 18, 1955, 1, available at Newspapers.com.

57. Ibid.

58. Giulio Andreotti, "The extraordinary La Pira," 30Days (30Giorni), February 25, 2004,
http://www.30giorni.it/articoli_id_3170_l3.htm.

59. "ITALY: Saintly Requisition," *Time Magazine*, February 28, 1955, The TIME Vault, http://content.time.com/time/subscriber/article/0,33009,861215,00.html.

60. Associated Press, "Italian Mayor Seizes Foundry, Turns Firm Over to Workers."

61. Associated Press, "Italian Mayor Under Fire Over Plant," *Indiana [PA] Gazette*, February 18, 1955, 23, available at Newspapers.com.

62. Ibid.

63. Associated Press, "Storm of Protest Gathers Over Seizure of Italian Plant," *Bridgeport [CT] Telegram*, February 18, 1955, 57, available at Newspapers.com.

64. Associated Press, "Mayor Of Florence Takes Over Mill, Stirs An Uproar," *Asbury Park [NJ] Press*, February 18, 1955, 32, available at Newspapers.com.

65. Associated Press, "Storm Rages Over Italian Mayor Who Seized Plant," *Petersburg [VA] Progress-Index*, February 18, 1955, 1, available at Newspapers.com.
66. Associated Press, "Plant Seizure By Mayor In Italy Is Protested," *St. Joseph [MO] News-Press*, February 19, 1955, 2, available at Newspapers.com.
67. Associated Press, "Italian Mayor Seizes Foundry, Turns Firm Over to Workers."
68. "James Ingebretsen; Ex-Chamber of Commerce Leader," *Los Angeles Times*, LAT Archives, March 18, 1999, https://www.latimes.com/archives/la-xpm-1999-mar-18-mn-18540-story.html.
69. Eckard V. Toy, "Spiritual Mobilization: The Failure of an Ultraconservative Ideal in the 1950's," *Pacific Northwest Quarterly* 61, no. 2 (1970): 77–86, www.jstor.org/stable/40488759.
70. James C. Ingebretsen, "For Reflection... with James C. Ingebretsen President Spiritual Mobilization," *McAllen [TX] Monitor*, June 26, 1955, 22, available at Newspapers.com.
71. Ibid.
72. Ibid.
73. Associated Press, "Mayor Saves Plant, Drums Up Business," *Birmingham [AL] News*, March 13, 1955, 28, available at Newspapers.com.
74. Marco Pietro Giovannoni, "Giorgio La Pira and the Sino-Italian friendship," Academia.edu, May 1 2017, https://www.academia.edu/35664337/Giorgio_La_Pira_and_the_Sino_italian_friendship.
75. Jon Talton, "Heyday for unions in the rearview mirror," *Seattle Times*, updated September 4, 2011, https://www.seattletimes.com/business/economy/heyday-for-unions-in-the-rearview-mirror.
76. Robert C. Doty, "Florence Unsure About Mayor; He is Called Saintly and Sinister," *New York Times*, June 26, 1964, 2, available at TimesMachine, timesmachine.nytimes.com.
77. Giorgio La Pira and others, *Philosophy of Communism* (New York: Fordham University Press, 1952).
78. Special to The New York Times, "Italian Leaders Arrive in Capitol: Scelba and Foreign Minister to See Eisenhower Today —Reds High on Agenda," *New York Times*, March 28, 1955, 1, available at TimesMachine, timesmachine.nytimes.com.
79. Ivan H Peterman, "Today's World - Italy Launches 10-Year Plan," *Philadelphia Inquirer*, April 1, 1955, 3, available at Newspapers.com.
80. Houston Harte, "Spreading the American Story: Information Service Giving Away Plenty, But Profits May be Huge," *Corpus Christi [TX] Caller-Times*, November 14, 1955, 18, available at Newspapers.com.
81. Ibid.

82. Ibid.
83. LaGumina J. Salvatore, Frank J. Cavaioli, Salvatore Primeggia, Joseph A. Varacalli, eds., *The Italian American Experience: An Encyclopedia* (New York: Garland Publishing Inc., 2000).
84. *Vermont History*, Vermont Historical Society, 46–47 (1978), https://vermonthistory.org/vermont-history-journal/.
85. "Firenze," *L'Informatore del Vermont New Hampshire e Maine*, November 26, 1955, 1, available at Newspapers.com.
86. Arnaldo Cortesi, "It Would Have Been Easy," *Salisbury [MD] Daily Times*, April 4, 1955, 6, available at Newspapers.com.
87. Arnaldo Cortesi, "Florence Seeks to Clear Slums: Loan Asked to Provide New Homes for Needy Craftsmen, Once the City's Glory," *New York Times*, March 29, 1955, 3, available at TimesMachine, timesmachine.nytimes.com.
88. Ibid.
89. Ibid.
90. Ibid.
91. Arnaldo Cortesi, "FLORENCE IS FULL OF U.S. TRAVELERS: They Find City Beautiful and Ramshackle, as Always— It Needs Funds Badly," *New York Times*, April 30, 1956, 18, available at TimesMachine, timesmachine.nytimes.com.
92. Robert E. Jackson, "Fascist Battle Police in Rome, Reds Are Quite on Election Eve: Italy Leaders Fear Apathy Will Aid Left," *Sacramento [CA] Bee*, May 26, 1956, 1, available at Newspapers.com.
93. Ibid.
94. Murray Edelman, "Sources of Popular Support for the Italian Christian Democratic Party in the Postwar Decade," *Midwest Journal of Political Science* 2, no. 2 (May 1958): 143–159.
95. United Press, "Christian Democrats Register Gains in Italy; Lose Control," *Elwood [IN] Call-Leader*, May 29, 1956, 4, available at Newspapers.com.
96. United Press, "Pro-West Bloc loses Full Grip on Rome, Right Holds Balance: Communist Slip in Major Cities But New Law Puts Fascist, Monarchist in Strategic Position," *St. Louis Post-Dispatch*, May 29, 1956, 1, 4, available at Newspapers.com.
97. Ibid.
98. United States Congress, House Committee on Appropriations, "Mutual Security Appropriations for 1956: Additional Hearings Before the Subcommittee of the Committee of Appropriations, House of Representatives" (U.S. Government Printing Office, 1955), 261.
99. United Press, "Electoral Laws Aid Italy Red," *Pottsville [PA] Republican and Herald*, May 29, 1956, 1, available at Newspapers.com.

100. United Press, "Italy's Christian Democrats Lose Control in Key Cities," *Racine [WI] Journal Times*, May 29, 1956, 7, available at Newspapers. com.

101. United Press, "In Italy: Christian Democrats Gain at Reds' Expense," *Santa Rosa [CA] Press Democrat*, May 29, 1956, 3, available at Newspapers.com.

102. Ibid.

103. Ibid.

104. Associated Press, "La Pira Named Mayor By 1 Year," *Clarksville [TN] Leaf-Chronicle*, August 4, 1956, 5., available at Newspapers.com.

105. Associated Press, "Wins Mayor Post Because Of Age," *Eureka [CA] Times Standard*, August 4, 1956, 11, available at Newspapers.com.

106. Associated Press, "Florence Mayor Wins Reelection Because of Age," *Boston Globe*, August 4, 1956, 2, available at Newspapers.com.

107. Associated Press, "Elected Mayor by A Whisker," *Mt. Vernon [IL] Register-News*, August 4, 1956, 1, available at Newspapers.com.

108. Associated Press, "La Pira Elected Again--By A Year," *Philadelphia Inquirer*, August 5, 1956, 3, available at Newspapers.com.

109. Associated Press, "Crusader Reelected," *Dayton [OH] Daily News*, August 5, 1956, 68, available at Newspapers.com.

110. United Press, "Mayor Monk Elected Again Thru A Quirk," *Escondido [CA] Times-Advocate*, August 8, 1956, 10, available at Newspapers.com.

111. "1957," "Giorgio La Pira, Servant of God: A Biographical Time-Line," Florin.

112. George Armstrong, "Fascism Tide Surges in Italy: Libel Suits Cited as Showing Activity." *Scranton [PA] Times-Tribune*, March 22, 1961, 8, available at Newspapers.com.

113. Anna Brady, "Italy Regime in New Peril: Florence Coalition Adds to Pressure on Government," *Baltimore Sun*, February 17, 1961, 4, available at Newspapers.com.

114. United Press International, "Nine Hurt in Florence Riot," *New York Times*, March 13, 1961, 10, available at TimesMachine, timesmachine. nytimes.com.

115. Armstrong, "Fascism Tide Surges in Italy."

116. Ibid.

117. Ibid.

118. Ibid.

119. Associated Press, "More & Soon Says Red Scientist," *New York Daily News*, April 13, 1961, 12, available at Newspapers.com.

120. Associated Press, "Reds Hint More Test Set If West Continues: Tass Repeats Soviet Ready To OK Pact Lag: In Blast Cited as Reason For Recent

Series," *Dayton [OH] Journal Herald*, November 6, 1961, 1, available at Newspapers.com.

121. Doty, "Florence Unsure About Mayor."
122. Ibid.
123. Ibid.
124. Associated Press, "Communist Mayor Resigns Position," *Abilene [TX] Reporter-News*, October 26, 1965, 32, available at Newspapers.com.
125. Ibid.
126. "The Great Arrival," Library of Congress, accessed June 8, 2021, https://www.loc.gov/classroom-materials/immigration/italian/the-great-arrival/.
127. Ibid.
128. "NATO's Traveling Exhibitions," NATO, accessed June 8, 2021, https://www.nato.int/cps/en/natohq/declassified_149236.htm.
129. Ibid.
130. Ibid.
131. Giorgio La Pira, Geneva, April 12, 1954.
132. "The city on the mount," Fondazione La Pira, accessed June 9, 2021, https://giorgiolapira.org/en/the-city-on-the-mount/.
133. Shala F. Maghzi, "United States Information and Educational Exchange Act (1948)," Encyclopedia.com, accessed June 8, 2021, https://www.encyclopedia.com/history/encyclopedias-almanacs-transcripts-and-maps/united-states-information-and-educational-exchange-act-1948.
134. "Impellitteri Trip Praised at White House; Rain Delays Mayor's Landing at Capital," *New York Times*, September 15, 1951, 4, available at TimesMachine, timesmachine.nytimes.com.
135. "MAYOR TO TAKE 3 OF STAFF TO ITALY: Mrs. Impellitteri to Have Nurse on 'Goodwill Tour' and Side Trip to Israel," *New York Times*, September 13, 1951, 24, available at TimesMachine, timesmachine.nytimes.com.
136. Associated Press, "Impellitteris Sail for U.S," *New York Times*, October 12, 1951, 8, available at TimesMachine, timesmachine.nytimes.com.
137. United Press, "Impellitteri in Florence," *Philadelphia Inquirer*, October 8, 1951, 20, available at Newspapers.com.
138. Robert D. McFadden, "VINCENT IMPELLITTERI IS DEAD MAYOR OF NEW YORK IN 1950's," *New York Times*, January 30, 1987, 36, available at TimesMachine, https://timesmachine.nytimes.com.
139. Mario Primicerio, email to author, January 13, 2021.
140. Richard Ehrman, "Italy City Fetes Man for Whom America Named," *Newport News [VA] Daily Press*, June 14, 1954, 8, available at Newspapers.com.
141. Ibid.

142. Associated Press, "1523 Visitor Recalled: Florence, Honoring Navigator, Greets 300-Year-Old New York," *New York Times*, February 1, 1953, 25, available at TimesMachine, timesmachine.nytimes.com.

143. Ehrman, "Italy City Fetes Man for Whom America Named."

144. Associated Press, "Florence Notes Vespucci Day," *Billings [MT] Gazette*, June 14, 1954, 1, available at Newspapers.com.

145. Associated Press, "Home Towners Honor Namesake Of Americas," *Albuquerque [NM] Journal*, June 14, 1954, 1, available at Newspapers.com.

146. Associated Press, "Italy Celebrates Vespucci's Birth," *Austin [TX] American*, June 14, 1954, 7, available at Newspapers.com.

147. Harry S. Truman, "Politicking in Italy Reminds Harry of U.S. Campaigns: This is another series of articles written especially for the Miami Herald," *Miami Herald*, May 30, 1956, 2, available at Newspapers.com.

148. Associated Press, "Truman Congratulates Italian Mayor on Win," *Boston Globe*, May 29, 1956, 2, Newspapers.com.

149. Harry S. Truman, *Off the Record: The Private Papers of Harry S. Truman* (New York: Harper and Row, 1980), 329.

150. United Press, "Florence Opens Closed Galleries To Harry Truman," *Bristol [TN] Herald Courier*, May 29, 1956, 11, available at Newpapers.com.

151. Associated Press, "Truman Congratulates Italian Mayor on Win."

152. United Press, "Truman Off for Venice," *Troy [NY] Times Record*, May 29, 1956, 18, available at Newspapers.com.

153. Truman, *Off the Record: The Private Papers of Harry S. Truman*, 330.

154. Associated Press, "Truman Congratulates Italian Mayor on Win."

155. "Italian Mayor Given Praise by Truman," *Chattanooga [TN] Daily Times*, May 30, 1956, 8, available at Newspapers.com.

156. Associated Press, "Truman Lauds Victor," *Pittsburgh Post-Gazette*, May 30, 1956, 6, available at Newspapers.com.

157. "Vacationing," *San Mateo [CA] Times*, October 30, 1962, 2, available at Newspapers.com.

158. Associated Press, "City of Florence Honors U Thant," *Rochester [NY] Democrat and Chronicle*, July 13, 1963, 11, available at Newspapers.com.

159. Lisa Reynolds Wolf, "The White Revolution in Iran," *Iran Review*, April 20, 2013, http://www.iranreview.org/content/Documents/The-White-Revolution-in-Iran.htm.

160. Associated Press, "Students Demonstrate Against the Shah of Iran," *Sacramento Bee*, February 11, 1964, 9, available at Newspapers.com.

161. New York Times News Service, "Shah's Visit To Spa Draws Protest," *Arizona Daily Star*, February 17, 1964, 21, available at Newspapers.com.

162. Ibid.

163. Ibid.

164. Associated Press, "To U.S. For Ceremony," *Kansas City [MO] Star*, October 10, 1964, 2, available at Newspapers.com.

165. "Italian Mayor to Join Parade Columbus Day," *Philadelphia Daily News*, October 10, 1964, 21, available at Newspapers.com.

166. "Mayor James H.J. Tate presents a proclamation," *Philadelphia Inquirer*, October 11, 1964, 93, available at Newspapers.com.

167. "10 Units Parade in Prelude of Columbus Day," *Philadelphia Inquirer*, October 12, 1964, 23, available at Newspapers.com.

168. Mario Primicerio, email to author, July 8, 2020.

169. Ibid.

170. Maurizio Renzini, "Thomas Merton and Giorgio La Pira: a Friendship for Peace," in *Universal Vision: A Centenary Celebration of Thomas Merton*, ed. Fiona Gardner, Keith Griffin, and Peter Ellis (Thomas Merton Society of Great Britain and Ireland, 2014), 50–57.

171. Associated Press, "Visiting War Graves," *St. Joseph [MO] Gazette*, October 7, 1952, 11, available at Newspapers.com.

172. Associated Press, "5th Army Vets Visited G.I. Graves in Italy," *Des Moines [IA] Register*, October 7, 1952, 2, available at Newspapers.com.

173. Associated Press, "Visiting War Graves."

174. Associated Press, "He's Out of One Army, Ready for Another," *Minneapolis Star Tribune*, April 14, 1953, 16, available at Newspapers.com.

175. Associated Press, "From Army to Army," *Hartford [CT] Courant*, April 15, 1953, 9, available at Newspapers.com.

176. Associated Press, "Dig up Solution to Tangled Case of US Bridegroom," *Montpelier [VT] Evening Argus*, April 13, 1953, 5, available at Newspapers.com.

177. Associated Press, "Italy Drafts Yank Newlywed, Frees Him in 20 Min. for U.S. Draft," *New York Daily News*, April 15, 1953, 42, available at Newspapers.com.

178. Associated Press, "Dig up Solution to Tangled Case of US Bridegroom."

179. Associated Press, "From Army to Army."

180. Reynolds Parker, "Anita Bridal Draws an Unbridled Mob," *New York Daily News*, May 23, 1956, 601, available at Newspapers.com.

181. Associated Press, "Anita Ekberg Married in Noisy Florence Ceremony," *Troy [NY] Times Record*, May 22, 1956, 1, available at Newspapers.com.

182. New York News Service, "Stars, Wedding Plans Delayed," *Spokane [WA] Spokesman-Review*, May 13, 1956, 2, available at Newspapers.com.

183. United Press, "Bare-Shouldered Anita, Ired Anthony Wed in Riotous Rite," *Arizona Republic*, May 23, 1956, 1, available at Newspapers.com.

184. New York News Service, "Stars' Wedding Plans Delayed."

185. Associated Press, "Anita Ekberg Married in Noisy Florence Ceremony."

186. Ibid.
187. Associated Press, "Florence Greets Queen Elizabeth with Pageantry," *Hartford [CT] Courant*, May 8, 1961, 34, available at Newspapers.com.
188. Fay Hammond, "Originality Marks Fashions Shown in Elegant Florence," *Los Angeles Times*, July 23, 1956, 63, available at Newspapers.com.
189. Ann Brewster, "Cinderella Story Is Full of Thrills for Hess's Teen-Trip-of-a-Lifetime Winner!," *Allentown [PA] Morning Call*, July 29, 1964, 32, available at Newspapers.com.
190. Ibid.
191. "Italy Enjoys Minneapolis Concert; Will Reciprocate," *Minneapolis Star Tribune*, June 22, 1952, 49, available at Newspapers.com.
192. Ibid.
193. Ibid.
194. Ibid.
195. Associated Press, "Denver Salute," *Austin [TX] American*, June 5, 1962, 4, available at Newspapers.com.
196. Bill Morgan, "Italian Mayor Host at a Reception For U-T Singers," *Greeneville [TN] Sun*, July 18, 1963, available at Newspapers.com.
197. Associated Press, "Florentines Fight Art Loan to U.S.," *El Paso [TX] Times*, October 19, 1956, 25, available at Newspapers.com.
198. Associated Press, "Suit May Block Sending of 40 Paintings to the U.S.," *Hartford [CT] Courant*, October 18, 1956, 2, available at Newspapers.com.
199. Reuters, "Italian Art Council Opposes Loan to U.S.," *New York Times*, October 23, 1956, 35, available at TimesMachine, timesmachine.nytimes.com.
200. Associated Press, "Suit May Block Sending of 40 Paintings to the U.S."
201. Reuters, "Italian Art Council Opposes Loan to U.S."
202. "Diplomas Awarded 402 H. S. Seniors: GHS Students Sound Theme of Democracy," *Galesburg [IL] Register-Mail*, June 4, 1954, 2, available at Newspapers.com.
203. Ibid.
204. "#Soul, Mario Primicerio ospite di Monica Mondo," Tv2000it.
205. David J. Krajicek, "Caryl Chessman became international crime celebrity in the 1950s when he was condemned to die for two sexual assaults," *New York Daily News*, May 24, 2014, https://www.nydailynews.com/news/crime/wrote-califonia-kidnapper-article-1.1803753.
206. Associated Press, "Chessman makes Last-Ditch Appeal: Court to Decide 2 Hours before Execution Slated," *Racine [WI] Journal Times*, May 1, 1960, 1–2, available at Newspapers.com.
207. Associated Press, "Execution of Red Brings Protest," *Fort Worth [TX] Star-Telegram*, April 22, 1963, 3, available at Newspapers.com.

208. "World: Death at Dawn," *Time Magazine*, April 26, 1963, The TIME Vault, http://content.time.com/time/subscriber/article/0,33009,830199,00.html.
209. Associated Press, "Execution of Red Brings Protest."
210. Giorgio La Pira, "A letter to his aunt Settimia Occhipinti," April 1931, Fondazione Giorgio La Pira, https://www.fondazionelapira.org/.
211. Roberto Ridolfi, *Vita di Girolamo Savonarola* (Florence: Le Lettere, 1981), 6th edition.
212. Linda Bordoni, "Pope: 'Politics is a commitment to humanity and holiness,'" Catholic
Media, November 24, 2018, https://catholicmedia.org/pope-politics-is-a-commitment-to-humanity-and-holiness/.
213. Maurizio Renzini, "Thomas Merton and Giorgio La Pira: A Friendship for Peace."
214. Reuters, "Tributes paid To Savonarola," *Spokane [WA] Spokesman–Review*, May 24, 1952, 2, available at Newspapers.com.
215. Mavro, "Girolamo Savonarola: Burnt by the Order of the Pope, then Sanctified 500 Years Later," Abrahamic Study Hall, January 31, 2019, https://www.abrahamicstudyhall.org/2019/01/31/burnt-by-the-order-of-the-pope-then-sanctified-500-years-later/.
216. Religion News Service, "Tells Parley of U.S. Link To Religion," *Des Moines [IA] Tribune*, July 25, 1952, 4, available at Newspapers.com.
217. Ibid.
218. Ibid.
219. Ibid.
220. Ibid.
221. Associated Press, "39 Countries Open Peace Congress," *Albuquerque [NM] Journal*, June 22, 1953, 15, available at Newspapers.com.
222. Joseph Lyons, *Clare Boothe Luce: Author and Diplomat* (New York: Chelsea House Publishers, 1988), 91.
223. Associated Press, "39 Countries Open Peace Congress."
224. Associated Press, "2nd Cultural Congress Opens in Italian City," *Arizona Daily Star*, June 22, 1953, 6, available at Newspapers.com.
225. "Prayer and Poetry," *Wichita [KS] Catholic Advance*, July 3, 1953, 10, available at Newspapers.com.
226. Kathleen Burke and Melvyn Stokes, *The United States and the European Alliance Since 1945* (New York: Berg Publishers, 1999).
227. Dr. Ronald D Landa, "CIA Covert Aid to Italy Averaged $5 Million annually from Late 1940's to Early 1960's, Study Finds," National Security Archive, February 7, 2017, https://nsarchive.gwu.edu/briefing-book/intelligence/2017-02-07/cia-covert-aid-italy-averaged-5-million-annually-late-1940s.

228. "Italian Red Hints at Vatican Offer: Says Agent Sought Soviet Pact on Religious Truce in '51 -Bid Called Unofficial," *New York Times*, May 19, 1953, 7, available at TimesMachine, timesmachine.nytimes.com.
229. "Italian Red Hints at Vatican Offer"
230. Ibid.
231. "Italian Says Gibe Met Bid to Soviet - Ex-Deputy Reports Russians Suggested Pope and Vatican Join Red Peace Partisans," *New York Times*, May 20, 1953, 8, available at TimesMachine, timesmachine.nytimes.com.
232. Ibid.
233. Arnaldo Cortesi, "Florence Mayor Inspires a Word: 'Lapirismo' Coined to Typify His Movement to Ease Humble Folks' Lot." *New York Times*, March 28, 1955, 6, available at Timesmachine, https://timesmachine.nytimes.com.
234. Arnaldo Cortesi, "Florence Mayor Inspires a Word: 'Lapirismo.'"
235. Ibid.
236. Ibid.
237. Ibid.
238. Ibid.
239. The Editors of Encyclopaedia Britannica, "Stefan Wyszyński," Encyclopaedia Britannica, last updated May 24, 2021, https://www.britannica.com/biography/Stefan-Wyszynski.
240. Associated Press, "Urges Churchmen Jailed by Stalin to be Released," *Hazleton [PA] Plain Speaker*, June 23, 1956, 3, available at Newspapers.com.
241. Ibid.
242. Associated Press, "Release of Churchman Sought," *Minneapolis Star*, June 23, 1956, 6, available at Newspapers.com.
243. Associated Press, "Suggests Russia Free Clergy Jailed Under Stalin Regime," *North Adams [MA] Transcript*, June 23, 1956, 2, available at Newspapers.com.
244. "Mayor Receives Letter from Poland Primate," *Wichita [KS] Catholic Advance*, February 1, 1957, 2, available at Newspapers.com.
245. Reverend James I Tucek, "Even Reds Love, Vote For La Pira: Humble Italian Mayor Demonstrates Real Charity of Christ," *Brooklyn [NY] Tablet*, June 30, 1956, 23, available at Newspapers.com.
246. Ibid.
247. Ibid.
248. Ibid.
249. Ibid.
250. See, for example, https://giorgiolapira.org/lattesa-della-povera-gente/.
251. Religion News Service, "Two Masses of The Poor are Offered Each Sunday: Mayor of Florence, Who Lives in a Monk's Cell, is Sponsor, Director

of Unusual Charity," *Brooklyn [NY] Tablet*, May 18, 1957, 29, available at Newspapers.com.

252. Ibid.
253. Ibid.
254. Ibid.
255. George Armstrong, "Distributes Madonna Cards: Italian Mystic Mayor Gives Russians Religion," *Boston Globe*, September 29, 1959, 6, available at Newspapers.com.
256. Paul Hofmann, "Italy Would Urge Khrushchev to Curb Red Parties in West," *New York Times*, August 17, 1959, 2, available at TimesMachine, timesmachine.nytimes.com.
257. Ibid.
258. George Armstrong, "Distributes Madonna Cards."
259. Ibid.
260. Ibid.
261. Ibid.
262. Ibid.
263. Ibid.
264. Ibid.
265. "St. Boniface Pupil's Letter to Magazine Wins Second Prize," *Sioux City [IA] Journal*, January 16, 1962, 14, available at Newspapers.com.
266. "Pope Paul Weighs Polish Visit," *San Francisco Examiner*, October 28, 1965, 16, available at Newspapers.com.
267. Ibid.
268. Richard Lachmann, "What American textbooks say about Vietnam, and about Americans' attitudes toward war," January 11, 2017, World Education Blog, https://gemreportunesco.wordpress.com/2017/01/11/what-american-textbooks-say-about-vietnam-and-about-americans-attitudes-toward-war/.
269. Diane Seo, "Getting Vietnam War Into Classrooms Is Still a Battle," *Los Angeles Times*, May 1, 1995, https://www.latimes.com/archives/la-xpm-1995-05-01-mn-61018-story.html.
270. David Kraslow and Stuart H. Loory, *The Secret Search for Peace in Vietnam*, 129.
271. Mario Primicerio, *Con La Pira in Viet Nam*, 71–73.
272. Reuters, "U.S. Maneuvers Puzzle Italian," *Spokane [WA] Spokesman-Review*, December 21, 1965, 15, available at Newspapers.com.
273. Ibid.
274. Gabriele Parenti, "La Pira, Ho Chi Minh, Vietnam: Primicerio's story," February 27, 2016, STAMP Toscana, https://www.stamptoscana.it/la-pira-ho-chi-minh-il-vietnam-il-racconto-di-primicerio/.

275. Associated Press, "Interpreter for Intermediary in Peace Feeler Assails Rusk," *St. Louis [MO] Post-Dispatch*, December 19, 1965, 30A, available at Newspapers.com.

276. Richard Dudman, "Nov.12 Hanoi Peace Move Reported Rejected by U.S.: Italians, American Lawyer Said to Have Been Intermediaries in Overture," *St. Louis [MO] Post-Dispatch*, December 17, 1965, 1, available at Newspapers.com.

277. Michael Sorkin, "Richard Dudman dies; he covered Vietnam war for the Post-Dispatch," *St. Louis [MO] Post-Dispatch*, August 4, 2017, https://www.stltoday.com/news/local/obituaries/richard-dudman-dies-he-covered-vietnam-war-for-the-post/article_f7c39296-dd94-5bfd-8aa5-e92ad915b6aa.html.

278. Richard Dudman, "Nov.12 Hanoi Peace Move Reported Rejected by U.S."

279. Ibid.

280. Ibid.

281. Ibid.

282. Ibid.

283. Ibid.

284. Ibid.

285. Ibid.

286. Ibid.

287. Ibid.

288. Associated Press, "Rusk Asks for Clarification of Hanoi 'Feeler' From Fanfani," *St. Louis [MO] Post-Dispatch*, December 17, 1965, 1, available at Newspapers.com.

289. Arnold H. Lubash, "Italian Ex-mayor Active 'Diplomat': La Pira's Reported Role in Peace Feeler Is Typical," *New York Times*, December 18, 1965, 3, available at TimesMachine, timesmachine.nytimes.com.

290. Ibid.

291. Associated Press, "Fanfani Reveals Details of Letter," *Spokane [WA] Spokesman-Review*, December 18, 1965, 12, available at Newspapers.com.

292. "205. Draft Memorandum From Secretary of State Rusk to President Johnson," Foreign Relations of the United States, 1964–1968, Volume III, Vietnam, June–December 1965, Office of the Historian, Department of State, accessed June 9, 2021, https://history.state.gov/historicaldocuments/frus1964-68v03/d205.

293. Ibid.

294. Associated Press, "Fanfani Reveals Details of Letter."

295. Ibid.

296. Douglas Kiker, "Hanoi calls Peace Bid U.S. Hoax," *Boston Globe*, December 19, 1965, 1, available at Newspapers.com.
297. Douglas Kiker, "Italian Reasserts Ho's Words," *Boston Globe*, December 19, 1965, 5, available at Newspapers.com.
298. Ibid.
299. Associated Press, "Italian Professor denies remarks blasting Rusk," *Lancaster [PA] Intelligencer Journal*, December 20, 1965, 31, available at Newspapers.com.
300. Robert C. Doty, "La Pira Sees Valid Basis," *New York Times*, December 20, 1965, 5, available at TimesMachine, timesmachine.nytimes.com.
301. Douglas Kiker, "Italian Reasserts Ho's Words."
302. Ibid.
303. Ibid.
304. M.S. Handler, "New York Lawyer Tells of Role as Transmitter of Hanoi 'Feeler,'" *New York Times*, December 19, 1965, 4, available at TimesMachine, timesmachine.nytimes.com.
305. Robert D. McFadden, "M.S. Handler, a Times Reporter Who Covered World War II, Dies," *New York Times*, February 11, 1978. 24, available at TimesMachine, timesmachine.nytimes.com.
306. M.S. Handler, "New York Lawyer Tells of Role as Transmitter of Hanoi 'Feeler.'"
307. Ibid.
308. Ibid.
309. Ibid.
310. Ibid.
311. Ibid.
312. Associated Press, "Lawyer tells of Relaying North Viet Peace Offer to Goldberg," *Boston Globe*, December 19, 1965, 29, available at Newspapers.com.
313. M.S. Handler, "Lawyer Meets Emissary: Yank Tells Role in Peace Bid," *Louisville [KY] Courier-Journal*, December 19, 1965, 24, available at Newspapers.com.
314. New York Times Service, "Lawyer Delivers Italian's Message," *Daily Oklahoman*, December 19, 1965, 10, available at Newspapers.com.
315. N.Y. Times - Chicago Tribune Service, "N.Y. Attorney Told of Ho's Peace Move," *Chicago Tribune*, December 19, 1965, 2, available at Newspapers.com.
316. Leo J. Wollemborg, "La Pira is Old Hand at Politics," *Boston Globe*, December 19, 1965, 29, available at Newspapers.com.
317. Ibid.
318. Ibid.

319. Ibid.
320. Ibid.
321. Ibid.
322. Donald Grant, "Latest Offer Similar to One Last October, UN Source Says: Halt in Bombing of North Viet Nam Reported to Have been Key to Negotiations," *St. Louis [MO] Post-Dispatch*, December 19, 1965, 1, available at Newspapers.com.
323. Ibid.
324. Chalmers M. Roberts, "Will Premature Disclosure of Offer Halt Peace Talks," *Spokane [WA] Spokesman-Review*, December 18, 1965, 12, available at Newspapers.com.
325. Associated Press, "Hanoi Peace Feeler is Branded a Hoax: Emissary Vows U.S. Killed Try," *Vernon [TX] Daily Record*, December 19, 1965, 1, available at Newspapers.com.
326. Drew Middleton, "Did U.S. Cool Peace Move?," *Nashville Tennessean*, December 19, 1965, 6, available at Newspapers.com.
327. Associated Press, "Hanoi Accuses U.S of Hoax: Italians Insist Ho Did Offer Peace Talk as He Reported," *Long Beach [CA] Independent Press-Telegram*, December 19, 1965, 2, available at Newspapers.com.
328. Associated Press, "But Minh Says 'Peace': Reds Say U.S. In Peace Hoax," *Alamogordo [NM] Daily News*, December 19, 1965, 1, available at Newspapers.com.
329. United Press International, "Hanoi Denies Leaders Made Peace Offers," *Casper [WY] Star-Tribune*, December 19, 1965, 2, available at Newspapers.com.
330. John M. Hightower, "Storm Over U.S. Report on Peace Bid," *Oakland [CA] Tribune*, December 20, 1965, 1, available at Newspapers.com.
331. Associated Press, "John M. Hightower, Reporter," *New York Times*, February 10, 1987, 54, available at TimesMachine, timesmachine.nytimes.com.
332. John M. Hightower, "Storm Over U.S. Report on Peace Bid."
333. Ibid.
334. Ibid.
335. Reuters, "U.S. Maneuvers Puzzle Italian," *Spokane [WA] Spokesman-Review*, December 21, 1965, 15, available at Newspapers.com.
336. United Press International, "Fanfani Criticized for Raising Hopes," *Casper [WY] Star-Tribune*, December 22, 1965, 7, available at Newspapers.com.
337. Robert C. Doty, "Pope Sends Please: Pontiff Exhorts Hanoi, Saigon, Washington to Pursue Peace," *New York Times*, December 26, 1965, 1–2, available at TimesMachine, timesmachine.nytimes.com.
338. Ibid.

339. Associated Press, "Fanfani Set to Explain Peace Feeler: Special Session Called to Hear of Role As Middleman," *Baltimore Sun*, December 27, 1965, 2, available at Newspapers.com.

340. Ibid.

341. Ibid.

342. Ibid.

343. United Press International, "Fanfani Quits Italy Job, Blames Viet Issue, Wife's 'Meddling.'" *Fresno [CA] Bee*, December 28, 1965, 4, available at Newspapers.com.

344. Reynolds Packard, "Italy Won't Let Fanfani Quit: Wife's Meddling Complicated Viet Move." *New York Daily News*, December 29, 1965, 56, available at Newspapers.com.

345. Ibid.

346. Associated Press, "Won't Reconsider: Fanfani Firm On Resignation," December 29, 1965, *Tucson [AZ] Daily Citizen*, 3, available at Newspapers.com.

347. Rufus S. Goodwin, "Fanfani Won't Reconsider His Resignation," *Casper [WY] Star-Tribune*, December 29, 1965, 2, available at Newspapers.com.

348. Associated Press, "Won't Reconsider: Fanfani Firm On Resignation."

349. Rufus S. Goodwin, "Fanfani Won't Reconsider His Resignation."

350. Reynolds Packard, "Italy Won't Let Fanfani Quit."

351. United Press International, "Fanfani Quits Italy Job, Blames Viet Issue, Wife's 'Meddling.'"

352. Rufus S, Goodwin, "Fanfani's Resignation Is Accepted By Moro," *Sheboygan [WI] Press*, December 29, 1965, 1, available at Newspapers.com.

353. United Press International, "Fanfani Rejects Plea to Stay as Italian Foreign Minister," *Coshocton [OH] Tribune*, December 29, 1965, 1, available at Newspapers.com.

354. "263. Memorandum of Telephone Conversation Between the Under Secretary of State (Ball) and President Johnson," Foreign Relations of the United States, 1964–1968, Volume III, Vietnam, June–December 1965, Office of the Historian, Department of State, accessed June 9, 2021, https://history.state.gov/historicaldocuments/frus1964-68v03/d263.

355. Mary McGrory, "How Globe Columnists See It: Fanfani Talked of Peace - - -That Started the Feud: Everybody's Mad at Everybody," *Boston Globe*, January 2, 1966, 93, available at Newspapers.com.

356. Ibid.

357. Ibid.

358. United Press International, "Italian Reds Demand Premiers Resignation," *Lincoln [NE] Star*, January 4, 1966, 14, available at Newspapers.com.

359. Associated Press, "Parties Back Policies of Italian Chief," *Salt Lake [UT] Tribune*, January 15, 1966, 8, available at Newspapers.com.

360. Matthew Continetti, "The Forgotten Father of American Conservatism," *The Atlantic*, October 19, 2018, https://www.theatlantic.com/ideas/archive/2018/10/russell-kirk-father-american-conservatism/573433/._

361. Russell Kirk, "To the Point: On Becoming a Fool in Hanoi," *Bridgeport [CT] Post*, January 13, 1966, 26, available at Newspapers.com.

362. Conversation with the author. See also the heading "1965" at "Giorgio La Pira, Servant of God: A Biographical Time-Line," Florin.

363. Associated Press, "Italian Official's Wife Dies," *El Paso [TX] Times*, September 26, 1968, 35, available at Newspapers.com.

364. David Dugas, "Protest in Florence," *Sacramento [CA] Bee*, April 1, 1967, 4, available at Newspapers.com.

365. Agence France-Presse, "Hanoi Negotiator and Pope Paul confer on Vietnam Peace," *Honolulu Advertiser*, February 15, 1973, 2, available at Newspapers.com.

366. United Press International, "Moro's party will run Fiat official as senate candidate," *Billings [MT] Gazette*, May 19, 1976. 12, available at Newspapers.com.

367. "1971-1973," "Giorgio La Pira, Servant of God: A Biographical Time-Line," Florin.

368. United Press International, "The Saintly Mayor," *Kittaning [PA] Simpson's Leader-Times*, December 12, 1977, 4, available at Newspapers.com.

369. Associated Press, "Giorgio La Pira of Italy, A World Peace Crusader," *New York Times*, November 6, 1977, 44, available at TimesMachine, timesmachine.nytimes.com.

370. United Press International, "The Saintly Mayor."

371. Associated Press, "Giorgio La Pira of Italy, A World Peace Crusader."

372. Ibid.

New City Press

New City Press is one of more than 20 publishing houses sponsored by the Focolare, a movement founded by Chiara Lubich to help bring about the realization of Jesus' prayer: "That all may be one" (John 17:21). In view of that goal, New City Press publishes books and resources that enrich the lives of people and help all to strive toward the unity of the entire human family. We are a member of the Association of Catholic Publishers.

www.newcitypress.com
202 Comforter Blvd.
Hyde Park, New York

Periodicals
Living City Magazine
www.livingcitymagazine.com

Scan to join our mailing list
for discounts and promotions
or go to www.newcitypress.com
and click on "join our email list."